Building Courageous Leaders
From War Room to Boardroom

by
Dale Collie
Major, US Army (Retired)

True North Publishing
Charlotte – Kiev – Vancouver – Beijing

Building Courageous Leaders
From War Room to Boardroom

ISBN: 978-1466207547

—Dedication—

Building Courageous Leaders is dedicated to our three sons and their wives who have been such a tremendous influence on me over the years

Page and Monetta Collie
Steve and Meredith Collie
Drew and Asher Collie

—About the Author—

As a professional speaker and author, Dale Collie uses the leadership skills of US Army Rangers to help key people succeed in tough times.

See p. 181 for details

CONTENTS

Preface

Laughter and wisecracks relieved the tension as the platoon leaders went back to their assigned areas. Tough work lay ahead, and we had no way of knowing whether we would see action before dawn. In spite of enemy gunners and incompetent pilots, we had survived this day, and that was good enough for now. (From Follow the Rules, *p. 87)*

Some people thrive on increased responsibility, calmly meeting every crisis, but others leave work feeling like GIs who have just survived a gunfight. For highly stressed leaders, the sound of the office door closing at day's end is as welcomed as the sound of the last explosion of a heated firefight. Survival is the name of the game for many leaders.

Customer deadlines, production problems, shipping errors, sales quotas, and administrative demands bring higher and higher stress levels. Initially, the accompanying adrenaline contributes to success, but prolonged adrenaline highs are detrimental, physically and emotionally.

Even for those most in control, the extended stressful periods promote forgetfulness and emotional turmoil. At some point, the dedicated performance of these leaders can be counterproductive; efficiency slows, and results are diminished.

Some leaders blame poor performance on inadequate equipment or weak business systems. Mature leaders, on the other hand, recognize that leadership development and proper training help overcome all of these problems. These same leaders know that good leadership requires courage —in the war room and in the boardroom.

Many military and civilian organizations have excellent programs for leadership development, but many make random and sporadic efforts following each crisis. A lot of money is wasted on unproductive programs that provide temporary results.

The responsibility for sound leadership development lies with the experienced leaders who make a continuous effort to guide others and find ways to refresh their own leadership skills.

Even when we recognize that we are not getting the desired results from our effort, our *busyness* or misplaced pride sometimes prevents our taking action to change things. Some of us have recognized our leadership deficiencies for years, but we are not motivated to get professional help to change things.

A review of the leadership traits discussed in this book is a good starting place for us and for subordinate leaders. Encouraging and motivating are big parts of leadership. Keep reminding your team members that it's never too late to be what they should have been.

The goals of this book are to:

- Refresh readers on essential leadership basics
- Provide compelling stories to launch discussion of these characteristics
- Motivate team members to participate in leadership discussions
- Encourage input from team members to gain their wisdom and participation in rejuvenating leadership

Success is often within reach if we only have the courage to do what we know should be done. It is the responsibility of every leader to guide subordinates and build courageous leaders who can succeed in the face of adversity.

Winston Churchill declared that courage is the most important of all human characteristics. Without courage the other characteristics are useless, and the lack of courage makes leadership qualities useless.

The stories included in this book are reminders of the topics and skills noted in the chapter titles. There are many other lessons to be gleaned from the stories. The title might just be a starting place for your own choice of topics. The Interactive Discussion Guide at the end of each chapter can be used to stimulate conversations if leaders want to use the stories as teaching tools.

Leaders need to be aware, however, that their own stories of success and failure are more compelling than these *war stories*. If you use this book as a teaching tool, let the conversations range through your group, and you'll learn from the participants' very own war stories and real life experiences.

From their own lives, each person can provide examples and anecdotes that are perfect for understanding leadership characteristics. You'll be impressed with your team.

Don't force the issue if team members fail to see examples of the leadership characteristic identified for discussion with each story. If the relationship is not apparent, team members might want to explain why the relationship does not work and then give examples and stories they think are better suited.

The events described here are intended for use as teaching points for corporate staff, families, and students. All of these stories are based on true events; objectionable dialogue and expletives are excluded for obvious reasons.

A glossary of military terms and slang is included on page 169.

Chapter 1

Safety
Jungle Waterfalls

Safety comes in cans—I can, you can, we can.

Anonymous

There are a million reasons for violating safety rules. Some of them are real killers.

Anonymous

Safety

Safety experts sometimes tell us that we are most vulnerable in new work environments or with new equipment. There are statistics to support this, and experience shows that we are just as vulnerable when engaged in routine activities.

Sure, the routine has the advantage of familiarity, but when the task is familiar, we sometimes become overconfident. New experiences encourage a certain caution that can deteriorate when *we know what we're doing.*

You can probably tell of your own experiences where accidents occurred because someone wasn't paying attention at home, in the office and factory, or on the highway.

While the military has a reputation of *doing things by the book*, their leaders are just as vulnerable to the hazards of routine.

The watchdog agencies such as OSHA might seem overbearing when it comes to safety, but the concept is good, and we should never scoff at someone who is trying to help us protect our most precious asset— people. Courage is required for leaders to demand compliance with safety policies, all the time. When it comes to safety, mavericks are not to be admired.

Jungle Waterfalls

Brushing the sweat from my forehead, I replaced my steel combat helmet and signaled, "Let's go." The company of infantry soldiers struggled forward through the bush for another hour.

For two days we moved through the jungle looking for signs of the enemy, but there were none. Our reconnaissance mission was a success so far, but a sense of danger had settled over the company during the past hour because of the deafening silence.

There were none of the jungle sounds that had become so familiar—no birds, no animal calls, no frogs, no nothing—just silence. None of the patrols reported signs of the enemy, but a high degree of alert was in effect.

It was almost time for a rest break when the point man asked that I come forward.

The request was routine, but a heightened sense of awareness caused me to move slowly and quietly. Creeping through the jungle, I stepped over and around each soldier who had taken up a defensive posture during the short stop.

When I caught up with the point man, the silence of the jungle was broken by the faint and continuous sound of rushing water. Without speaking, the point man led me still farther. We stopped and he used his rifle barrel to pull back the limbs in the thick jungle growth. I took three steps forward, and the view was phenomenal.

To the right, the jungle opened widely around a towering waterfall. To the left, a beautiful pool of water mirrored the jungle canopy, and a stream thirty feet wide tumbled across the rocks downstream.

"Looks like a travel brochure," he said. "How about a swim, Captain?"

"Looks like a giant ambush site to me," I replied. "No swimming allowed."

On my signal, the four platoon leaders came forward to get a visual reconnaissance of our situation. Each of them had an opinion about how we should do the river crossing, and none of them took into account the dangers involved.

"That's enough talk," I said. "We're doing a formal river crossing because Charlie could be waiting in ambush—over there on the other side of the river or up there on top of the falls."

-Take your time-

One platoon leader countered, "We haven't seen the VC for three days out here. Ain't gonna be no ambush."

Another chimed in with, "My troops are working hard enough just walking through this jungle. It'll take more than an hour to get set up for a real river crossing."

"Captain, we're dead tired. How about if we just send a squad to the other side to see if they draw fire?"

"Drop it," I ordered. "Dead tired and dead are two different things. Do you want to write and tell one of your soldier's moms that her son is dead because we were too tired to do things right? We're going to secure the entire area before we cross.

"To help you remember that point, your platoon has the honor of climbing up the side of this mountain and securing the top of the waterfall."

"Yes, sir," he responded and took a step back.

"Second platoon, you're going downstream to secure our left flank. Go down there about fifty meters and set up a machine gun to cover the other side. Send a patrol out another fifty to a hundred meters beyond. They'll stay out there as a listening post until we radio them back for the crossing.

"Third platoon, your job is to set up a rear guard while we're hanging around here. When we're ready to cross, you'll go over first and scout out the other side.

"Mortar platoon, you set up a defense right here along the river to guard our front while everyone else is getting into place. I want you to guard the tree line over there and put some guys in position where they can see the top of the falls from here.

"Now, listen up, everybody. You tell every soldier that we're not stopping for water when we cross this river. This is a very dangerous place. After everything is secure, we'll send patrols to the river to get water.

"Got that? Any questions?

"OK. Let's go," I concluded.

One platoon moved to the left flank to explore downstream. Another took up rear guard, and the third platoon began a wide swing around to the right, climbing a steep bluff to a position above the waterfall.

A long while passed before the climbing platoon radioed success in reaching the top of the waterfall. More time passed while they negotiated the riverbank.

The platoon leader finally radioed, "Six, we've got both sides covered up here. You oughta see this."

"I can see you up there. Are you bragging about the scenery, or is there some sign of Charlie?" I asked.

"It's a good thing we took our time with this one, Six. It looks like the VC just pulled out. We have one squad climbing higher up the mountain to cover our position, and one squad is moving upstream. Do you want anything else?"

"What kind of signs did you find?" I asked.

"The leaves and limbs are mashed down like they've been hiding up here awhile—two positions, maybe two or three VC in each. Looks like a machine gun tripod was stuck in the ground with a bead right down there where you are. The marks are fresh!"

With a feeling of relief, I keyed my radio and said, "Roger, roger—send out those squads and hold your position to cover our crossing.

"Can you get across the river up there?" I asked.

"Roger," was his reply.

"OK. After we've all crossed down here and have a secure site over there, you make your crossing up top and climb down to meet us."

The platoon leader responded with the quick acknowledgment, "Roger."

The downstream squad reported no enemy signs, and I gave them a similar order: "Set up your machine guns to cover both sides of the river and prepare to guard our crossing.

"Point squad," I directed, "cross the river here. It looks shallow enough to wade across. Watch out for booby traps as you come up out of the water. Don't use the path as you enter the wood line over there. Signal me after you've moved a hundred meters into the jungle, and we'll follow."

"Roger," came the answers, and the company went into action.

After both riverbanks were secured, a team from each platoon filled canteens with fresh water. Scouting patrols covered new ground beyond the river as we waited for the rear guard platoon to join us. RTOs notified artillery that we would not need their support this time, and the sound of the waterfall was soon left behind.

As the day went by, several GIs commented on the missed opportunity to wash off layers of dirt and grime.

"Sure would have been nice to go skinny-dipping back there," said one soldier.

"Right," said another. "It's been about a week since I had a bath of any kind."

None of them were so bold as to actually complain about the situation, but these teenagers let me know how good it would have been to play in the water.

In the late afternoon, circumstances brought the point man and me together once again. There was some small talk and conversation about plans for the night and the next day.

"Whatcha say I walk point tomorrow?" he asked.

"That's up to your platoon leader," I replied. "Why do you want to walk point again?"

"I like working for a boss who is willing to go the extra mile for the sake of safety. Thanks for being so careful back there at the river, Sir."

I turned to leave his position and was almost out of earshot when I heard his parting question, "Say, Captain, where'd you learn to do a river crossing?"

Since time didn't permit a conversation on this subject, I simply smiled and said, "US Army Ranger School."

(For the details that I did not explain to the point man, see chapter one of *Frontline Leadership*.)

-Interactive Discussion Guide on Next Page-

Safety

-Interactive Discussion Guide-

The following questions are intended to stimulate conversation about the story and the noted topic. Participants are encouraged to provide their own experiences and anecdotes to strengthen the discussion.

1. What was the outcome of the captain's precautionary strategy at the river crossing in *Jungle Waterfalls*?

2. Would the outcome have been different if the captain had ignored his awareness for additional precaution?

3. Should leaders always follow established safety procedures, or can they sometimes rely on their vast experience to know that all is well?

4. Do you have any personal examples of benefiting from following detailed safety procedures? Do you have examples of those who ignored the procedures?

5. Are there situations in your organization that need additional attention to safety? Explain.

6. Does your organization have a system that encourages making recommendations on safety issues? If you could change safety policy or unsafe conditions in your organization, what would you recommend?

7. With whom will you share these thoughts to help you focus on success and sharpen your ideas?

—Notes—

Chapter 2

Know the Competition
Counterfeits

*People in the same trade are
always competitors.*

Chinese Proverb

---

*Know your enemy as you know yourself and
you can fight a hundred battles with no
danger of defeat.*

Chinese Proverb

Know the Competition

The importance of knowing the competition should rate pretty high on a leader's priority list. While some managers understand a great deal about the competitors, many only know the competitors' names and products.

Outside the sales and product development departments, many managers fail to grasp the importance of competitor information in their department: operations, accounting, customer service, communications, IT, etc. Each of these managers can contribute to organizational effectiveness by researching the competition, but only a few managers actually consider the importance of this type information.

Similarly, many managers incorrectly identify their primary competition. Some fail to see *small* players as a major threat; others miscalculate the importance of new technology and new products that will replace their own line of goods and services.

A good leader should know the strengths and weaknesses of each competitor as well as they know their own company. They should understand details about such things as suppliers, sources, processes, costs, and management structure.

Research should include an in-depth analysis of the suppliers and the entire chain of influencing factors on the competitors' supplies: the cost of raw materials and availability, the influence of international currency exchange, consumer forecasts, weather trends, political impact, and so on.

To make the information useful, it must be analyzed and then distributed to all of the leaders involved. The facts are useless without the analysis, and none of it is of value if no one knows about it.

Regardless of how much information is collected, the most important thing to know about the competition is who is shooting at you and which competitor you need to have in the sights of your rifle.

Counterfeits

"Ohhhhhh, Tiger Valley? That's a real bad place, Captain," said the executive officer. "We went out there one time, before you came. Bad! Bad! Bad!"

"Well, headquarters just briefed us on a big, three battalion operation for Tiger Valley—starts day after tomorrow—big hammer and anvil operation. They still think they can hunt the Viet Cong like tigers are hunted in India.

"Personally, I think the VC will boogie up over the mountains and escape the valley when our troops move through the valley. If there's a big training base out there, the bad guys are going to suspect a blocking force at the south end of the valley. They won't fall for this old trick."

"I know," said the executive officer. "They didn't fall for it last time, either."

"This is a big secret," I explained. "The villagers will tell the VC if they get word of the operation, so we're telling the troops that we're going in the other direction—just to prevent any slip of the lip."

The executive officer paused and leaned back against a jeep before he responded. "Captain, do you want me on the operation, or can I take care of things for you right here? I've got only three more weeks in this country, and I'd hate to spend that time in Tiger Valley."

"The honchos have a lot of intelligence information about the valley," I said, delaying my answer to his question.

"Bunch of Viet Cong out there with North Vietnamese troops training them. There's even a rumor of some Russian advisors mixed in that command."

After a significant pause, I told him, "You stay here at LZ Bayonet, Lieutenant. You've had enough field time. I want you to work with the platoon leaders after I give them an operations briefing. Help them get the supplies we need for a ten-day field trip. Make sure we have food we can eat cold. It wouldn't do for us to light up cooking fires after we sneak in there and set up this supposedly secret blocking position."

"Yes, Sir, yes, Sir, three bags full," laughed the lieutenant. I thank you! My wife thanks you! My kids thank you! My mom and dad thank you!"

"All right, LT. That's enough of the thanking. If you'll stop dancing around we can brief the troops."

-More than 300 US and South Vietnamese Soldiers-

The briefing for our company's platoon leaders was much like that of the brigade briefing officer, except for the actual destination, of course.

To cover our area of responsibility, additional troops were assigned to our company—a reconnaissance platoon from our own battalion and a ranger company from the South Vietnamese Army—about 150 extra soldiers for a total of approximately 300.

The tactical plan established a staging point where the reconnaissance platoon and Vietnamese ranger company would rendezvous to receive supplies—food, ammunition, and clean uniforms—before joining our company

-D-day minus one-

The South Vietnamese ranger company made radio contact several times the afternoon before the troop movement. Delay after delay constantly changed the plan, and I had an ongoing radio conversation with the reconnaissance platoon leader who was moving into position at the rendezvous point.

The entire arrangement made me nervous because I wouldn't be able to brief the Vietnamese soldiers until we were actually on the ground, up there in the high valley where we were supposed to sneak into position and hide out until the enemy came running into our fortified perimeter.

The recon platoon leader was getting nervous about the delayed arrival of the South Vietnamese soldiers. They wanted to receive their supplies and move out of their position before dark. They correctly assumed it was too dangerous to spend the night at a location so easily identified by the enemy.

An hour before sunset, I radioed the platoon leader. "Call off the rendezvous. We'll make plans for the ranger company to join you when the helicopters pick you up tomorrow morning."
The platoon leader answered my call. "The ranger company just arrived," he said.

I hastily interrupted, using his call sign to get his attention, "Shooting Star, this is Blue Six. Have you made contact with their commanding officer yet?"

"Roger, roger, Six. He's standing right here beside me. Speaks pretty good English, too. Over."

"Shooting Star, put the handset next to your ear so only you can hear me. Over."

"Roger, Six. What's up? Over."

"Tell your squad leaders to pick up their radios so no one else can hear. I'll explain in my next transmission. You should move away from the ranger commander as you do this. Over."

Moments later, "Roger, Six. We're ready, but I have a lot of work to do here. The ranger company is starting to distribute their rations and ammo. What's the big secret? Over."

"Star, those guys in your camp—I don't know who they are. They might be VC. The ranger company is still at LZ Bayonet. I want you to have every squad leader calmly assemble his men at one side of your perimeter. Don't tell the troops what's up. Take your weapons and radios, but leave everything else in place. Move them all toward your position.

"Somebody might panic, and you're going to lose a lot of men if you start a firefight inside the perimeter. If those are good guys, this won't hurt a thing. If they're bad guys, they'll try to get away when they see what you're doing. Can you do this, Star? Over."

"Roger. My squad leaders have been listening. They're moving now. The GIs are wondering why they have to move out. Over."

After a moment's pause, my radio came to life again, "Blue Six, Blue Six, the rangers picked up their ammo and food and are moving to the other side of the perimeter. Over."

-Keep your troops together-

"Roger, Star. Stay where you are. Pull your squads into a small perimeter around you and be ready in case you get attacked. If they are VC, they might have more bad guys behind you, or they might circle for an attack. Do not divide your platoon. Over."

"Roger, Six. We're just about set, and those guys are moving away to the north. They sure look like South Vietnamese. They even have ranger patches on their uniforms. Over."

"Star, we've been on the battalion net talking with the ranger company commander while you're talking to

34

me. He's still at LZ Bayonet. You've just resupplied the enemy! Over."

Silence from the other radio gave me an eerie feeling, and several moments passed before I called back to the platoon. Darkness was upon us by that time.

"Star," I radioed, "Collect the remaining gear and move out toward your preplanned night defensive position. Is there any chance the VC picked up a marked map or found out your planned night position somehow?"

"Negative, Blue Six. They didn't get any maps, and we'll put out a rear guard to make sure we aren't followed."

"Send out some scouts to make sure you aren't ambushed right outside your perimeter, Star, and switch all your radios to alternate frequency Alpha right now. If the VC got your frequency, we'll leave them behind when we change."

The own RTO requisitioned more supplies for the real ranger company that was still at LZ Bayonet.

The night was uneventful, and the real ranger company arrived with the first flight of helicopters the next morning. The recon platoon leader made an early request that his name be left out of the report on last night's incident; then we all went to Tiger Valley.

As I write about these events thirty years after the war, I envision a couple of aging Viet Cong veterans together in a small village near the South China Sea, having a little rice and crawfish dinner and a final smoke before sundown.

One of them says to the other, "Huang, I was thinking today about the time we put on the enemy uniforms and went into the American camp over there by Phui Bong. That was about the easiest resupply we ever had! The young Americans were foolish to let us walk into their camp."

And Huang, slapping at a mosquito, laughs lightly and replies, "You're right, Chan. I remember that night. I remember carrying around all that ammunition that wouldn't fit our rifles. And I remember the next day when you had diarrhea from eating that can of green eggs and ham!"

As the two of them laugh again, darkness slips down over the ancient village just as it has done every evening over the centuries. The Americans are gone, and the Vietnamese remain to tell stories of the old days.

-Interactive Discussion Guide on Next Page-

Know the Competition

-Interactive Discussion Guide-

The following questions are intended to stimulate conversation about the story and the noted topic. Participants are encouraged to provide their own experiences and anecdotes to strengthen the discussion.

1. The enemy in *Counterfeits* had an agenda different from what the Americans expected. What measures could have been taken to prevent enemy infiltration of the reconnaissance platoon?

2. Were the leaders correct in their decisions when they began to suspect the infiltration? Should things have been done differently?

3. Discuss your own experiences with information about the competition. Does your company systematically collect competitive information?

4. Are there advantages to gathering, detailed in-depth competitive information in civilian organizations? Examples.

5. Are there situations in your own organization where hidden agendas might be detrimental to the success of the group?

6. What measures can your organization implement to learn more about the value of gathering competitive information, analyzing it, and acting upon it?

7. With whom will you share these thoughts to help you focus on success and sharpen your ideas?

—Notes—

Chapter 3

Who Gets the Credit
Missing in Action

Egotism is the art of seeing things in yourself that others cannot see.

Anonymous

Back of every noble life there are principles which have fashioned it.

G.H. Lorimer

Who Gets the Credit

The desire for personal credit sometimes overwhelms a leader's good judgment, and opportunities for personal recognition can get in the way of maximum performance.

Both the military and the corporate world have a reputation for harboring those with an unrelenting quest for self-promotion; each has its fair share of egomaniacs. Young leaders who pursue rapid promotions can be found in almost every venue, and their motivation is generally financial gain or personal power. In their midst are the honest leaders who willingly serve others for the success of everyone.

Detailed personnel evaluations provide more than enough information to identify the rogues, but quarterly successes typically outweigh all other considerations. Upper management and CEOs are frequently influenced by the bottom line because that's where they, too, are measured.

If the mavericks are not controlled and taught by those at the top of the management pyramid, their headlong quest for personal achievement will go unchecked—and the organization will suffer.

It is the responsibility of good leaders to retrain or redirect those who advance their own cause regardless of their negative impact on the organization and other people.

Missing in Action

The room was hot; the meeting was unnecessary, and the officers were tired. Our thoughts were not on the subject, but on our own companies as the battalion operations officer droned on about administrative concerns.

Three of the four company commanders were present, and the fourth could be heard approaching on the gravel path.

Just as the operations officer commented on the enemy body count for that week, the screen door banged open, and the fourth company commander stepped from the bright sunlight into the shaded room. His company had just returned from an extended operation in the mountains, and his appearance revealed the difficult conditions they had endured: dirty and torn uniform, long hair, unshaven face, and a cloud of dust hovering around him.

Actually, he looked pretty normal to those of us who had companies in the field, but the neatly uniformed operations officer took exception to his appearance.

Gruffly, the ops officer said, "Captain, you're not in the jungle anymore. Get cleaned up before coming to the meeting."

Undeterred, the captain stood his ground and shot back, "I heard you giving the body count when I came in. How many did you say were killed?"

The ops officer, a major, objected to the captain challenging his authority.

"I gave you an order, Captain. The body count is none of your business right now."

The captain smiled and held in the air a burlap sack he had brought with him. His boldness commanded silence in the room. With a sharp movement, the battle-weary captain turned the sack over and laughed aloud as several human skulls rolled across the wood flooring.

He stopped laughing, and silence returned as the skulls came to rest on the planks.

No one could respond through the shock of the event. The disheveled captain finally said, "Whatever the body count is, put down six more for my company!"

Before the major could gather his thoughts, another officer asked, "What happened?"

"Ahhhhhh. We were waiting up there on the ridge for the choppers to bring us back here, and one of my guys stepped in a hole. He got to looking around and found these six skulls lying just inside the entrance of this collapsed bunker. It looked like a bomb or artillery shell got 'em all. We couldn't tell how long they'd been there, but only the skulls were in the bunker. No weapons. No bones."

Instead of taking up the issue of this guy carrying around a sackful of skulls, the major missed the point and returned to the subject of body count. "Why do you think you get the count? Artillery should get it."

"Nope," said the captain. "I'm sure artillery didn't know these guys were dead. They haven't been counted, and they wouldn't be yet if my company hadn't spent three weeks up in the mountains. Now, what do we do with these body parts?"

To rescue the rogue company commander from the impending harangue, another company commander responded, "Put them back in the sack and go get cleaned up. I'll call the morgue and ask the officer in charge of the dead."

Within minutes of the conversation, I returned to my company by helicopter and was caught up in the ongoing stress of field command. The circumstance of the skulls was never made known, and it is unclear as to whether any action was ever taken against the company commander. I'm not even sure what action should have been taken. The strain of combat had warped his sense of humor, and he couldn't understand why the rest of us didn't see the humor in the bag of bones.

Keeping score of dead soldiers on a blackboard and bragging about the growing numbers is bizarre enough, but dragging around a bag of skulls and laughingly spilling them onto the floor are sure signs of battle fatigue.

There is no way to know how long those skulls had been on that mountainside—months, perhaps, or years—or whether they had been killed by Americans or by the French before us.

The Vietnamese soldiers who entered that bunker were more than chalk marks on a blackboard. They were six young Vietnamese men who felt that the bunker gave them some security. They were the sons of now grieving mothers, the husbands and boyfriends of young women who waited in vain for their return, and the fathers of babies who would know of them only from faded pictures.

Not one of these things was discussed that late afternoon at LZ Bayonet. Instead, the question that filled the air was, "Who gets the credit?"

-Interactive Discussion Guide on Next Page-

Who Gets the Credit

-Interactive Discussion Guide-

The following questions are intended to stimulate conversation about the story and the noted topic. Participants are encouraged to provide their own experiences and anecdotes to strengthen the discussion.

1. In *Missing in Action,* what seemed to motivate the officer who dumped the skulls on the briefing room floor?

2. Was the response of other officers appropriate?

3. Did the major handle the incident properly? Were alter- natives more appropriate?

4. What has been your own reaction to those who want to advance themselves in spite of the consequences to others? Examples?

5. Have you experienced situations in your own organization where people are rewarded at the expense of someone else's job, career, or reputation?

6. What can good leaders do to retrain or redirect those who care more about themselves than the organization?

7. With whom will you share these thoughts to help you focus on success and sharpen your ideas?

Chapter 4

Tend to Your Business
Look Out for the Tree

Plans get you into things, but you have to work your way out.

Will Rogers

Fools are in a terrible, overwhelming majority, all the wide world over.

Henrik Ibsen

Tend to Your Business

With years of emphasis on management by objectives, quality control, and six-sigma, it seems that America's entire workforce would be focused on efficiency and productivity. The possibility of someone goofing off in the workplace just seems contrary to the tenets of modern management.

Considering the serious nature of their mission and the hazardous equipment they handle, the military should be even more focused on their work. Military personnel, however, are much like civilians in their tendency to act foolishly when they should be paying attention to their duty assignment.

Civilian jobs should be safer than military jobs, but the number of corporate casualties I've seen is almost as great as those I saw in the army: crushed hands and feet, broken arms and legs, severe burns, fatal falls, toxic inhalation, overturned vehicles, cuts and concussions, food poisoning, eye injuries, hearing loss, and amputations. Most of these problems could have been avoided if the employees had simply concentrated on the task at hand.

These physical injuries take a toll on the corporate bottom line, but there is an even greater monetary loss involved in the way employees waste time while on the pay roll. Those side conversations on the telephone or in person are expensive. Extended lunch breaks, late arrivals, early departures, gripe sessions, gossip, and sports talk also take their toll on the bottom line.

Corporate policies and strict management encourage safer and better performance, but in the end, every employee must take it upon themselves to tend to their own business.

Look Out for the Tree

During the period of half-light, just before sunrise, tired soldiers slipped into our company perimeter. Without speaking, they dropped their rucksacks and gave attention to their weapons. Another night of full alert had ended.

Their faces were still blackened with the night camouflage, and their uniforms were wet from dew and sweat. They were weary, but no more so than the rest of the company and no more so than they had been on any other recent morning. At least the night had been quiet.

The announced strategy was that our infantry company would saturate the valley with ambush sites each night and that we would rest during the day. The reality of the situation, however, was that we pulled ambush duty each night and then spent the daylight hours patrolling much of the same territory, scouting villages, following up on directives from battalion staff, receiving ammunition and supplies, and performing a dozen other essential activities.

Our only period of relative calm was between dawn and the time we moved out for the day's activities. Each morning was kind of a celebration—the sun was coming up, and everyone was alive. None of us knew what the day would bring.

Canteen water provided a hasty shave, and the day was officially started with a quick breakfast of cold C-rations —green eggs and ham. A returning squad leader noted my breakfast and created a couple of lines that might be found in one of Dr. Seuss's nonsensical poems about such delicacies. "Would you like them here or there? Green eggs and ham are everywhere!" he laughed.

Interrupting the attempted levity, the radio operator held a handset in the air and announced, "Phone call, Captain."

"This is Blue Six," I responded.

"Top o' the morning to you. Did y'all have a nice night's sleep?" said our universally disliked battalion operations officer. The major had a certain skill for being obnoxious, and his morning greeting was made on our company radio frequency rather than the battalion frequency he should have used. His intention, of course, was to harass everyone in our company who carried a radio.

The RTO glanced in my direction and asked, "Which is worse—waking up to green eggs and ham or getting a visit from battalion before full light?"

-Pop smoke-

Before I could respond, the voice on the radio announced, "Pop smoke, Blue Six. We're inbound."

"Smoke's out," replied my radio operator as he casually pulled the safety pin from a smoke grenade and threw it into the clearing.

The helicopter pilot radioed, "I see white smoke. Is that you?"

The RTO ignored the sloppy radio procedures and confirmed the color of the smoke. A light observation helicopter, the kind used by news teams and traffic control, quickly touched down.

I jogged across the clearing and stood waiting just outside the danger of the whirling blades for the major to dismount. The engine continued at a high rpm, and the operations officer threw open one of the doors. He waved anxiously for me to come near and held out one arm as though to shake hands when I approached the aircraft.

He was smiling as I stepped onto the skid, but this was no greeting. When he grasped my hand, he pulled me toward the entry and yelled, "Get in! Get in!"

The engine noise increased as the pilot lifted off. This was no time for me to resist. I dropped into a seat just behind the major and adjusted the seat belt. By the time I was handed an aviation helmet wired for internal communication, we were well away from my company.

"Where are we going, Major?" I asked.

"We're gonna do a little reconnaissance. We're flying the river looking for Charlie."

More than a little surprised, I asked, "Hey, Mr. Pilot, can I call my company with this headset mike?"

"Roger that. Just key the mike. We're on your company push, but don't announce on the radio what we're doing. We think Charlie is monitoring these frequencies, and we don't want him to know we're flying the river."

Disregarding the somewhat naïve remark, I contacted my radio operator on the ground and asked him to relay a message to the leader of first platoon. "I'm going for a ride. Take command until I get back." He acknowledged my order with a simple "Roger, roger," and I returned to the intercom.

A quick check of my rifle confirmed that the ammo magazine contained a full twenty rounds. I felt incompetent as I considered the danger of going on such an escapade with such a small amount of ammo.

The pilot held the small helicopter close to the treetops and dropped even lower when he came to natural clearings in the foothills. We approached the river along a small tributary.

Then we swept north, twisting and turning with each river bend, flying just above the level of the water.

I had flown just above the treetops many times in Vietnam, but this was my first experience at flying below treetop level since my first days in the army at Ft. Knox. I had avoided such offers because the Ft. Knox experience ended with my witnessing a tragic crash of two fully loaded helicopters. My own error caused me to miss being aboard one of the helicopters that day, and pilot error caused the crash. Would today be the same?

Our early morning adventure was undertaken to catch unsuspecting Viet Cong along the riverbank as they bathed or filled canteens. There was no way to hide the sound of helicopters flying nap-of-the-earth, but the sound was distorted so that a listener couldn't easily discern the direction of flight.

After twenty minutes or so, I was ready to return to my company. I thought the river recon strategy to be ineffective, and I was concerned about my company's preparation for the day's planned operations.

"How far are we going, Major?" I asked.

-Pay attention-

Without answering, the major said into the intercom, "Look at that, boys! Three deer."

Abruptly, the pilot pulled the aircraft to the right and tilted the right side of the helicopter toward the ground. We were circling a small clearing in the jungle, just above the trees.

Our angle of flight prevented my seeing directly below us, but I could hear the excited remarks of our operations officer. And I saw him push the barrel of his M-16 through the now open window beside him.

As the pilot circled in a tight flight pattern, the major fired single shots at the deer. Having no experience at shooting from a moving helicopter at panicked deer racing in all directions, the major had no luck. He finally put his selector switch on full automatic and fired bursts of five to seven rounds.

The panicked deer continued to jump about the meadow, unaware that they could flee the clearing and escape.

"Take it up on the other side and let the captain have a shot," said the major.

Without a word in response, the pilot twisted the controls so that we were circling to the left. We were flying almost on our side, so my angle of fire was straight down. When I delayed opening my window, the major gave me an order.

"You shoot those deer, Captain. We're not going back without a body count of some kind."

Tentatively, I opened the window and fired a couple of ineffective shots.

"Put it on full oughta-get-'em, Captain. Can't you shoot any better than that?" harangued the major.

To respond to this criticism, I had to look upward, over my right shoulder. As I turned my head, I saw through the front windshield that we were headed directly for a large, dead tree.

"Look out for the tree!" I shouted.

The pilot jerked the joystick from the extreme left to the extreme right. Shifting his feet on the pedals and manipulating the stick, he caused the helicopter to invert itself. Almost immediately, we went from a position where my left window was facing the earth to a position where it faced the sky.

The skids of the chopper slashed through the tree leaves as we went past. The tree slipped past beneath us.

Again, I could see through the front windshield, and it was clear that we were headed right into a hillside. The pilot wrestled with the controls. A split second later we cleared the brush covering the hill.

A hard right turn brought us back toward the river, and we dropped down below tree level as we again approached the clearing. The deer were still running about the open area.

The once-excited major was somewhat subdued after the two near accidents, but it was clear that the pilot was taking us back for another potshot at the panicked creatures.

Into the intercom I said, "Major, I've had enough of the deer hunt. I only have a few rounds of ammo, and I need to get back to my company."

-Hunt's over-

"Aw, you're all the same. We get on the trail of something worth shooting, and you run out of ammo," he complained. He turned toward the pilot and said, "Take us on back to his company site."

Within minutes, we approached my company position. I said to the pilot, "I'm glad you missed that tree back there."

"What tree?" he laughed. "I didn't see no tree; tell your troops to pop smoke."

In the coming days, I saw this pilot often as he flew in my area of operations, but I refused to ride with him for any reason. I would rather walk than ride with a pilot who paid more attention to deer hunting than he did to flying, a pilot who was prone to pilot error.

Likewise, I always made sure I understood the major's intentions before I came near his aircraft. We spoke the same language, but his definition of recon was a whole lot different than mine. I felt that I might need an interpreter to distinguish other words that carried different meanings.

The major almost succeeded in getting a body count that day. Sometimes, I wonder how the telegram to our families would have been worded if the pilot had been less agile in handling the helicopter. Would it have carried reference to a big tree or a looming hillside? Would it have commented on the deer hunt? Or, would it have declared that we had met our end, bravely serving our country while conducting reconnaissance operations in search of the elusive Viet Cong?

-Interactive Discussion Guide on Next Page-

Tend to Your Business

-Interactive Discussion Guide-

The following questions are intended to stimulate conversation about the story and the noted topic. Participants are encouraged to provide their own experiences and anecdotes to strengthen the discussion.

1. Were the key players in *Tend to Your Business* paying attention to their assigned mission? Explain the actions and events that support your position.

2. Which leader was responsible for maintaining focus on the business at hand? What should this leader have done differently?

3. What alternatives did the subordinate leader have after he became involved in the misguided actions?

4. Have you witnessed situations in your own organization where people or equipment were endangered due to a lack of attention to business?

5. Can you identify situations that could get out of hand without frequent emphasis on correct procedures or safe operations?

6. Are there currently situations in your organization that need management's attention to get things back on track?

7. With whom will you share these thoughts to help you focus on success and sharpen your ideas?

Chapter 5

Get All the Facts
Bomb Fragments

Now what I want is facts; facts alone are wanted in life.

Mr. Gradgrind in Charles Dickens' *Hard Times*

Get All the Facts

One of the most common errors in the military and in business is the failure to get the pertinent facts before taking action.

- Salespeople sometimes launch into presentations without gathering information about what their prospective customers need.
- Customer Service sometimes fails to get essential information needed to solve difficult situations.
- Lack of appropriate information causes many operations managers to insist on established procedures rather than adapting to customer needs.
- CEOs sometimes act on partial information, causing unnecessary confusion and expense.

Almost all managers could benefit from using a standard checklist of information to solve problems. The basic requirements are often overlooked because someone *thinks* they understand the situation or because they are reluctant to *appear foolish* for asking basic questions. As often as not, the missing information is the result of ignorance, poor attention to detail, overconfidence, or lack of concern.

One of the most embarrassing situations results from leaders who direct changes without having all the information.

Likewise, many employees provide insufficient information unless required to answer the questions who, what, when, where, and why with plenty of emphasis on the *why*. You can't ask too many *why* questions. For example, a late delivery might deserve the following kinds of *why* questions.

Q. Why did the shipment arrive late?
A. We didn't ship on time.

Q. Why didn't we ship on time?
A.   The order wasn't ready.

Q. Why wasn't the order ready?
A. We didn't have some of the parts.

Q. Why were the component parts not on hand?
A. There was trouble on the production line.

Q. Why did the production line have trouble?
A. One of the machines broke down.

Q. Why was the machine improperly maintained?
A. We don't have a maintenance schedule.

Bomb Fragments

"Sit down and relax a few minutes," I told my radio operators. "We'll give the scouts another half hour before we break camp."

"These scouts never find anything, Captain," responded the artillery forward observer.

"Well, we're waiting for them to report that they find nothing. More than once, Charlie has ambushed grunts as they left their well-defended night positions."

Turning away from the radio operators, I sat on the ground, leaned back against a tree trunk, and spread a map sheet across my knees.

"When you finish that call report, I want to show you some terrain features on this map," I said to the company RTO.

As he sat down beside me, a call came in from the leader of the first platoon, which was patrolling a river just to our north.

"Blue Six, Blue Six, this is Blue One, over."

"Whatcha got there, Blue One?"

"Well, what we've got here is a bomb in the riverbed," said Blue One.

Finding unexploded bombs wasn't really a surprise. We didn't actually expect to find something like this, but dealing with it was a matter of routine. This type incident was more common in some areas than others, and we had a standard operating procedure for blowing such shells where they were found.

We respected the trained ordinance teams who defused this type ammunition, but seldom were they available to take care of these problems in the rice paddies and jungles where we operated.

"This bomb is kinda short, partially buried in the sand of the riverbed," reported the platoon leader.

"I'm gonna guess it's a two hundred-pound bomb. Should I go ahead and wire it for detonation?" he asked.

-Blow it up-

Actually, the only decision to be made at this point was how to dispose of the bomb. Leaving the bomb for the enemy to use in making booby traps was out of the question.

For this size bomb, our procedures called for molding plastic explosive around the nose cone. A blasting cap was then inserted into the explosive and a hand-held electric generator was attached. The standard wire was one hundred feet long, and the platoon leader objected lightly as I told him to increase the distance between himself and the bomb.

"String three wires together; make it three hundred feet, and make sure your entire platoon takes cover behind the riverbank," I explained. "You don't know how much bomb is buried in the sand. When you're ready to blow, we need to alert the rest of the company."

Time passed as he worked on the project, and my eyes were drawn back to the map. Minutes passed. As I tried to memorize the lay of the land for the day's maneuvers, I actually forgot about the first platoon's bomb in the river.

And the platoon leader forgot about us as he nervously prepared the bomb for detonation. He forgot to tell us he was ready to blow it up.

When he fired the detonator, the explosion was tremendous. The mountain shook. Leaves fell from the trees around us. We were momentarily deafened.

At my location, no one moved. Thoughts of tragedy ran through my mind—was the explosion an accident? Were our troops injured? A tree limb above us rustled again as a chunk of the bomb fell from the sky, landing squarely on the map sheet I'd been analyzing and coming to rest right between my knees.

The radio operator and I stared at each other in disbelief as I cautiously moved away from the bomb parts lying before me. And the radio crackled to life with a one-word explanation from the platoon leader —"Oops."

My pride and the map were the only things damaged, but the whole incident could have been avoided with a little more research. It should have been easy to determine that the platoon leader was dealing with a two thousand-pound bomb instead of a much smaller two hundred-pound bomb. His original plan to use a detonating wire of only one hundred feet would have brought certain death.

On that exciting day and frequently afterwards, the radio operator who sat beside me that day was present as we discussed operations. Whenever he felt like a plan was incomplete or foolhardy, he simply interjected a quiet "Oops."

If he sensed that his leaders were not considering all the facts, he persisted by asking, "How big's the bomb, Captain?"

When the embarrassed patrol leader returned to our command position, the reception was mixed. He didn't know whether he should apologize, and I didn't know just how much he deserved to be chewed out.

How do you reprimand someone who clearly failed to get all the facts but has barely escaped death, knowing just how fortunate he was?

-Interactive Discussion Guide on Next Page-

Get All the Facts

-Interactive Discussion Guide-

The following questions are intended to stimulate conversation about the story and the noted topic. Participants are encouraged to provide their own experiences and anecdotes to strengthen the discussion.

1. Who was responsible for gathering all the facts before exploding the bomb in *Bomb Fragments*?

2. Who is ultimately responsible that subordinate managers gather all the facts – in the story and in your organization?

3. How does one learn to delay final decisions until all the information is considered?

4. Have you made decisions in your personal life that would have been different had you gathered more information?

5. Have you experienced situations in your organization where decisions and actions were premature?

6. Does your organization have procedures to ensure sound decision-making? What could be changed?

7. With whom will you share these thoughts to help you focus on success and sharpen your ideas?

-Notes-

Chapter 6

Preventive Maintenance
A Poke in the Eye

If you take care of your machine, your machine will take care of you.

If you take care of your people, your people will take care of you.

Anonymous

Preventive Maintenance

Preventive maintenance is costly, but not nearly as expensive as postponing regularly scheduled services.

Organizations that schedule routine preventive maintenance programs for their equipment, programs, and people are rewarded with dependability, loyalty, and long-term success.

Just as critical is the preventive maintenance for personnel. Traditional leadership and communication strategies help develop employees who are happy and productive on the job. As with scheduled equipment inspections, annual medical physicals are a key component.

But just as important are things like keeping employees informed, seeking employee input, attention to personnel needs, vacation schedules, and all the other things people need to be healthy and happy.

No matter what the size of the corporation, good leaders emphasize balanced preventive maintenance programs for all of their assets—people, programs, and equipment.

A Poke in the Eye

"Arghhh," growled the private, attempting to avoid a scream of pain. He dropped his rifle, covered his left eye with both hands, and bent over as he moaned loudly.

"What happened? What's wrong?" asked other GIs crowding around the wounded soldier.

"Arghhh, my eye, my eye, my eye," repeated the injured teenager.

The medic pushed his way through the small group on the mountainside and took charge.

"Set him down," he directed. "Hold his arms and legs so I can get a look at his eye."

The soldier's eye had been injured by a tree limb that was pushed aside by the GI in front of him as we made our way through the jungle. The sergeant in the lead had lost his balance and prematurely released the limb without warning. The limb slashed across the soldier's cheek, cutting the skin deeply and slicing the white area of his left eye. Blood covered the young soldier's face as his hands were pried from the wound. The cut on his eye was gory.

The medic wasn't afraid of blood. Compress bandages were placed on the skin wound to stop the bleeding, but he didn't know the procedure for dealing with such a wound to the eye. To make matters worse, we were too far from headquarters to make radio contact with our short antennas. A long-wire antenna was required, and it takes some time to set up such a contraption.

As the seriousness of the injury began to unfold, I knew we would have to change our immediate plans.

"Listen up, platoon leaders. We're staying here for a while. First platoon, you take the north side; second platoon you take the east. Third platoon will take the south, and fourth the west. Set up outposts with radios a hundred meters out so we don't get surprised here. Also, send out patrols in your assigned area. Have them look for a landing zone for a helicopter. Put the rest of your platoons on perimeter," I ordered.

The injured soldier rejected the morphine shot offered by the company medic. As time passed, the pain lessened, but the message we finally received from the battalion doctor was that we should evacuate the soldier for care in the division hospital.

"Good idea, Doc," I responded. "but we have no LZ near here. Can you get us a medivac helicopter with a jungle penetrator?"

The doctor readily agreed, but within thirty minutes he radioed to let us know that the request was denied.

-Equipment Failure-

"They have maintenance problems with the jungle penetrator," he said. "The retractor is broken. They can drop the seat through the jungle canopy, but they can't pull your guy back into the helicopter."

"Doc, are you saying that our division has only one medivac helicopter equipped with the penetrator? What are they thinking about back there?"

"That's the best I can do, Captain. I'm no mechanic, and the division commander takes exception to my telling him how to equip the division. You're getting no medivac, over."

"Roger that, Doc," I responded. "But there are no landing zones anywhere around here."

The GI was unable to open his injured eye and sat in the leaves holding a gauze patch over it. Even though we had moved to the top of a small plateau, he became concerned about the company's safety as we paused in this precarious location. He wasn't angry with the sergeant who had released the tree limb, but the sergeant felt tremendous guilt that he had injured one of his own men.

While the rest of the company knew of our peril in this location, all of them were willing to do whatever was necessary to make sure we got the proper care for the young man. Everyone knew that we would want maximum effort if any of us were in his position.

My own concern was twofold. First, what steps should I take to protect the company as a whole and continue our mission? Secondly, how could I get adequate care for the wounded soldier?

If the company moved out in pursuit of our mission, we would have to disconnect from the long antenna and lose contact with the doctor at our battalion headquarters. If we stayed with the antennas, we would lose valuable daylight in moving toward a defensible night position.

-Let's go, Captain-

After another hour had passed, the GI wanted us to continue our mission in spite of his pain, and the doctor finally agreed, telling us that evacuation was impossible.

The patrols converged on our position, and the long antennas were retrieved. Contact with our battalion headquarters was broken.

As we moved forward, everyone was very careful about the tree limbs. The platoons were happy that we would not be stuck on the side of that mountain for the night.

The radio operators keyed their handsets from various points along our trail, trying to make contact with headquarters. The injured soldier gritted his teeth and cupped a hand over his bandaged eye.

Even though the wounded GI was mobile, there were many other things to worry about: what we would do if we made contact with the Viet Cong since we had no radio contact, no artillery, no priority for medivacs, no landing zones in this jungle, no way to fix an injured eye.[1]

On the mountainside that day, there were no answers to any of these questions. All of us knew that better planning could have prepared us for this unfortunate incident. Preventive maintenance would have kept that jungle penetrator ready for action. Attention to our programs would have improved radio communications, and better training would have taught the injured GI to avoid such accidents by not following so closely.

-Interactive Discussion Guide on Next Page-

---

[1] The GI suffered with this eye wound for two more days before he could be evacuated. Eventually, his eye healed without complications.

Preventive Maintenance

-Interactive Discussion Guide-

The following questions are intended to stimulate conversation about the story and the noted topic. Participants are encouraged to provide their own experiences and anecdotes to strengthen the discussion.

1. What was the commander's main concern when the soldier was injured in *A Poke in the Eye*?—Mission accomplishment, maintenance, personnel, etc?

2. Could preventive maintenance for equipment have changed the situation on that day? Could training and preventive maintenance have helped avoid the situation?

3. Have you experienced a work environment where disciplined preventive maintenance programs affected the success of the organization? Were these programs focused on equipment or on people?

4. How do you rate the preventive maintenance program for *equipment* in your organization— nonexistent, poor, good, excellent? What could be done to improve the current situation?

5. How would you rate the preventive maintenance schedule for *people* in your organization? What could be done to improve the current situation?

6. How would you rate the preventive maintenance program for *programs* in your organization? What could be done to improve the current situation?

7. With whom will you share these thoughts to help you focus on success and sharpen your ideas?

Chapter 7

Don't React—Think About It
Hold Your Fire

Appearances are deceptive.

Anonymous

Things are not always what they seem.

Anonymous

Don't React—Think About It

When stymied by new situations or unexpected obstacles, young officers are often ordered to "Do something, Lieutenant. Don't just stand there."

The objective is to help lieutenants learn to make decisions quickly because combat is unforgiving. Hundreds of decisions are required in a time of crisis, and these new leaders must learn how to assimilate the information, determine how their actions will impact the unit and the mission, and act quickly to continue. Pausing at the wrong time can be a deadly decision in warfare.

With all this emphasis on quick decision-making, the lieutenants must concurrently learn to think through their decisions because things are not always what they seem.

Corporate leaders continuously confront similar situations, and it is sometimes difficult to teach young leaders how to balance this feat. The military has the advantage of live action training, whereas most corporate training takes place in the business itself.

In preparation for the *real thing*, lieutenants are challenged with using troops and weapons to accomplish realistic missions. Problems and obstacles are built into the training environment. Cadre and higher ranking officers grade the exercise, and repetition is required until everyone knows just how to get the job done.

Historically, corporate practical exercises have been impractical, but some innovative leaders have found ways to simulate and train using live-fire situations.

- Salespeople are confronted with various obstacles in simulated meetings with purchasing agents.
- Purchasing agents are taught research and negotiating skills in life-like situations.
- Customer service personnel develop professional techniques for helping customers and dealing with problems.
- Accounting managers learn to be alert for error-causing situations and to systematically solve problems.
- Manufacturing sometimes trains in a real-life environment, so new leaders can detect and solve problems they will see in the future.

Two of the key elements taught in each of these situations are that decisions need to be well thought out, and they need to be made quickly.

Premature decisions cost employees and organizations a lot of money. Proper decisions, on the other hand, provide positive results in the lives and well-being of employees and the corporation.

Hold Your Fire

Just inside the tree line, our patrol stopped. I removed my helmet, quickly wiped my eyes, and slipped the heavy combat gear back into place. It was completely dark by this time, but the temperature still hovered above a hundred degrees.

The quarter moon was of little help even though the sky was clear. We were accustomed to night combat, and our eyes had to adjust to the deeper darkness of this wooded area.

Patrols like ours were scattered across the broad valley in an effort to prevent enemy infiltration and rocket firings toward a nearby American installation. Gunfire a few hundred yards to our south told us one of the patrols had encountered the enemy. The sounds of battle were followed by the sound of the company radio reporting the situation.

"Blue Six, I guess you heard the gunfire. We ran into Charlie right where we were going to set up for the night."

"Anybody hurt?" I responded.

"Naw. It was just one guy. He ran off to the north on the paddy dike. I don't think we got him," said the lieutenant. "One more thing," he added. "Charlie dropped a pistol when he ran."

"Leave that pistol right where it is," I ordered. "It might be a booby trap."

"Roger that," said the squad leader. "We'll mark the spot and set up somewhere else. I'll call in when we settle down."

Soon, we heard footsteps running toward us in the night, and I thought, "This is an unlucky night for you, Mr. VC. You're running from one ambush right into another."

To my own patrol, I ordered, "Take cover. It looks like he dropped his weapon, but we don't know for sure."

Except for the steady sound of the running VC, there was silence. The rhythmic sound of his bare feet at this distance from the other gunfight made me think that he must be in good shape physically. Would he run right past us in the dark? Would he be tired and walk quietly by the time he reached us?

We waited silently. Just when we expected to see him in front of us, limbs shook like crazy on a bush nearby. We heard no more running. Had he collapsed?

It was too dark to see whether the enemy soldier had stopped to rest or whether he resumed walking quietly on the trail. Since peripheral vision registers images in lower light than does our direct line of sight, we tried all the tricks, looking left and right of the bushes, scanning above and below where I thought the enemy might be. Just when we thought we had him in our sights, he blended in with the night.

Combat experience had taught us to make sure of what was going on before we took action, so the GIs held their fire. They knew that rifle shots would reveal our positions. The muzzle flash of the M-16 rifle is bright at night and immediately makes the shooter a target in the dark.

Throwing a hand grenade would have been a better choice, but we didn't know where the guy was. There we sat, thinking we were pretty smart to have our ambush in just the right place but wondering how to handle the situation with the enemy concealed nearby.

-Where's the enemy?-

One of our GIs swore he could see the VC sitting near the trail. Another said he was ten yards farther to the right. I didn't think either of them saw the Viet Cong. "Hold your fire," I whispered.

Moments passed and limbs rattled on a bush near the original site. Then limbs moved on another bush several feet in the other direction. I wondered whether this one guy had turned into two people. Maybe the sound of running had actually been two men running in step with each other.

Had the VC discovered that we were nearby? Was he trying to lure us into firing?

The noise occurred again, much nearer this time. Was the enemy crawling toward our position? Slowly, I slid the safety lock to *fire* and pointed my rifle in the direction of the sounds. If close combat was upon us, I wanted to be ready.

Silence. Look this way and that. Shift my weight, so I might spring up if need be.

Without warning, the bush next to me shook noisily. Reflexes took over and I turned to face the enemy.

. . . . .

To my embarrassment, the enemy turned out to be a four legged critter of some kind. The rodent had fallen from a tree limb into the bush by my side—lucky for both of us that I didn't shoot the creature.

We had been ready for a fight. We were anxious to capture the VC we'd heard running in the night. Our rifles were ready, and our adrenaline was up. But the enemy soldier was gone and we were left with a small animal.

GIs laughed quietly when they discovered my predicament, but the dropped pistol was no laughing matter.

Fortunately, the first patrol left the pistol alone until it could be examined in daylight. It was booby-trapped, and one of our young soldiers would have died if the patrol had been too anxious to claim its prize.

The next day also brought an examination of the runner's easy-to-follow footprints.

While it was impossible to know for sure, it appeared as though the running VC knew the exact location of both the first patrol and our ambush position. His tracks showed that he hid behind a rice paddy dike after he got near our position, then crawled some distance away before standing and walking on in the night.

We never determined the purpose of this runner. He had planted the booby-trapped pistol on the trail and then alerted the first patrol, hoping that one of them would pick up the weapon and blow himself up.

Maybe his purpose in running right up to our ambush site was some kind of a daredevil prank; maybe it was a challenge of sorts between rivals after drinking too much of the Vietnamese tiger beer. Perhaps the true VC plan was foiled when we held our fire.

Whatever the purpose of the runner, an important lesson was reinforced for us that night—hold your fire until you see the whites of their eyes. Everything is not as it seems.

-Interactive Discussion Guide on Next Page-

Don't React—Think About It

-Interactive Discussion Guide-

The following questions are intended to stimulate conversation about the story and the noted topic. Participants are encouraged to provide their own experiences and anecdotes to strengthen the discussion.

1. Did the soldiers in *Hold Your Fire* have enough good information on the enemy to safely fire their weapons?

2. Did the soldiers take proper actions? Should they have taken an alternative approach?

3. Have you experienced situations in the workplace where urgency was required but there was too little information to make a good decision? Explain what happened and what actions were taken.

4. What are the consequences of having insufficient information about your company's resources? Have you seen opportunities lost because your organization acted with insufficient information?

5. Does your organization have procedures for training all employees on the resources and tools available to them? Are they effective? Identify procedures that might be implemented to train employees in good decision-making.

6. How can your organization increase its effectiveness by using tools, technology, or training that helps leaders quickly make good decisions?

7. With whom will you share these thoughts to help you focus on success and sharpen your ideas?

Chapter 8

Follow the Rules
Turn Loose

"It's not wise to break the rules until you learn to follow them."

T. S. Eliot

The Golden Rule – The one with the gold makes the rules.

Anonymous

Follow the Rules

Unwritten policies are the norm in smaller organizations where management often prepares formal, written policies only to comply with legal requirements.

More formalized rules and policies are established by larger companies to guide the organization. Compliance with these established policies is important to efficient management.

While some might disagree with company policies and consider violations to be insignificant, good leaders insist upon strict compliance to avoid the negative impact that always follows such actions. No matter how illogical the *bureaucracy* seems, it is important to follow the rules.

Turn Loose

As the pilot took the map from my hand, I keyed the intercom mike and said, "The target village is marked in red.

"We're going to cordon that ville tomorrow, and we want a fly-over recon at ten thousand feet."

"We can do it. Is this a one-ville mission or do you want to go somewhere else?" asked the pilot.

"Before we get there, fly over a decoy village and three more after the target. You pick 'em."

"Got it," he said. "Sit back and enjoy the ride."

The mission could have been accomplished without the chopper ride, but the aerial reconnaissance helped all of us understand what we had to do since this operation would take place in total darkness using radio silence.

We sat on the chopper floor, just behind the pilot and copilot. Two door gunners rode just behind us, managing M-60 machine guns to take care of business if we got into a fight.

"That's village number one," said the pilot. "We'll circle to the right and the next ville is your target."

"Roger, circle right," I responded into the microphone.

Five minutes later, we approached a second village. With one hand I held my M-16 rifle, and with the other I touched each of the platoon leaders to get their attention. "Listen up. Next ville is the target. We're going to circle right, so move over here to look out this door."

-Here's what we're going to do-

The platoon leaders were soon observing their areas of responsibility.

"Second platoon, do you see that little hill we marked on the map? That's where you'll split off from the company and come in from the south. Move up to that bunch of trees on the south side of the village and wrap around toward the east. Cover the ville all the way up to that little creek.

"First platoon, after second platoon splits off, you'll swing around to the north. Circle in there from that bunch of trees all the way down to where second platoon will meet you by that little creek. You have responsibility for the creek itself.

"Third platoon, fill in the difference from the northwest side in those trees, down to second platoon on the south side. You two link up at that patch of pine trees down there.

"Now, you guys need to identify the troops that will be linking up with the platoons on either side. Make sure they know each other. We want a tight little circle around that ville, and we don't want anyone slipping through your perimeter.

"There won't be any moonlight tonight, so give them some signals to work with—no lights and no noise. We'll be moving into position after 0300 hours, and the villagers shouldn't know we're visiting until dawn when they start out to their rice fields.

"The command group will be with the mortar platoon on that little island just north of the village. We'll follow second platoon when they move up there to go around the north side of the ville. Any questions?"

Everyone nodded or held up a thumb to show that they understood. The helicopter leveled off and headed toward another village.

In passing over the additional villages, we hoped the villagers would take us to be rear-area brass on a sightseeing flight. If they did suspect a cordon, they would have no way of knowing which village was the real target.

The pilot circled two more villages and turned toward the last in the series. As we neared the collection of grass huts, I noted that we weren't making a broad sweep around the edge of the village; instead, we were making a tight turn directly above it. The pilot seemed to be in a hurry to get back to his rear-area activities.

When I keyed the mike to comment on his sloppy work, my remark was interrupted by the unmistakable sound of bullets hitting the helicopter. The chopper shuttered as the bullets perforated the bottom of the aircraft.

Immediately, the helicopter nosed over into a vertical dive —straight toward the rice paddy below us.

For a few seconds, I expected the pilot to level off or to maneuver into position for autorotation. More than once, I'd been on choppers that had to land without full engine power, and each time, the pilots had caused the blades to rotate in a way that would slow the descent and give a rough but safe landing.

There was no sign of autorotation. We were going in nose first at sixty miles an hour.

I checked my rifle to make sure I had a full magazine of twenty rounds, and I said a prayer, fast. The ammo was for the enemy who would surely swoop upon us, and the prayer was to keep us from swooping on them.

When the paddy was right before us, the helicopter vibrated tremendously and the metal frame made stressful noises as the pilot pulled the bird out of the dive and into level flight just above the green fields.

At that instant I could tell we would not crash, but a few more seconds passed before I realized that the three men seated on the floor were holding onto my arms and legs. None of them realized they had taken hold of me as a survival reaction, and we seemed to be frozen in that moment in time.

"Turn loose. Turn loose. Everything's all right," I said, shaking arms and legs to break their hold. Their suntanned faces were pale white. They turned loose but stared into my eyes looking for assurance.

Before we could react further, the pilot's voice sounded in my intercom headset. "Radio your company and get ready for us to sit on the ground while we inspect the damage," he said.

Radio connection was made at once with the mortar platoon leader who had been left in charge of the company on the ground. He was anxious to help as I told him, "Pick a landing zone and put troops around the perimeter. Don't use the same LZ we left from. We'll be there in twenty minutes, and the pilot wants to do a little maintenance inspection before leaving."

"Roger that," said the platoon leader unquestioningly.

-Check the damage-

Minutes later, the landing skids touched the ground and we quickly jumped off. One of the door gunners was ordered to inspect the damage while the engine continued at high rpm. They wanted to lift off in a hurry if there was more gunfire.

The platoon leaders jumped from the helicopter and ran quickly toward the tree line, not really knowing where their platoons were but understanding well enough that they wanted to be away from that helicopter.

I paused to survey the ten bullet holes that lined the hull. None seemed to make a critical strike, and it was amazing that we had taken so many rounds without anyone being wounded.

The rounds passed through the bottom and lodged in the interior or passed all the way through the upper structure. The holes appeared to be the size made by heavy machine guns, a favorite of the Viet Cong in these villages and a weapon powerful enough to easily knock helicopters out of the sky.

The various controls seemed to meet the pilot's approval as he moved the levers and pedals. Then the door gunners waved briefly as the helicopter took flight. There was no radio communication as the pilot left for home.

"Thanks for running the company while we were gone," I told the mortar platoon leader.

"Well, thanks for the thanks, Captain, but I'm not looking for a promotion. I'm glad you're back," he replied.

The platoon leaders briefed their men on the upcoming action and prepared for the night operation. When they gave orders just before dark, everything seemed surreal. The platoon leaders and I had the same feeling of camaraderie that we experienced after gunfights, and we realized that we had once again been at death's door.

The pilot was in full control during the daring dive, which we knew by now was an evasive maneuver to avoid taking further hits.

He had succeeded in making the enemy think the helicopter was fatally hit, and we took no rounds after the first volley.

We agreed that this was a smart evasive technique, but the more we talked about the event, the more we realized what a terrible pilot we had.

He had circled directly above the village instead of skirting around the edges. Someone noted that our altitude must have been well below our requested ten thousand feet elevation. It's not easy to hit a moving aircraft with a heavy machine gun at that distance, almost two miles.

Instead of complimenting our pilot on a good escape, we concluded that he should be punished for endangering our lives. If he had followed our standard operating procedure for flying recon, we would have been out of range of the machine gun. But the conversation was cut short by the approaching darkness. I broke up the pity party with an abrupt order.

"Listen up. We want twenty-five percent guard duty tonight instead of the usual fifty. Nobody moves outside their platoon position until we're ready to pull out of here at 2030 hours (8:30 p.m.).

"We've got about six hours, so your troops need to sleep early. I want that cordon in place by 0300 (3.a.m.), so we'll be moving fast and not sleeping again until tomorrow night.

"Keep radio silence from now until daylight. We'll use runners to communicate since we're all so close together. When you're in place at the village, I want you to personally check both ends of your perimeter to make sure you are linked up properly. I want one hundred percent alert once we move in on that ville. Nobody sleeps until the sun goes down tomorrow.

"When you're set up, key your radio mike once, twice, or three times according to which platoon you are. It's my responsibility to catch your signal. Give me the signal before 0300 hours.

"That ville is going to be a regular circus tomorrow. The colonel has medical and dental teams and a big food giveaway. You'll have to answer to him if anyone gets out of this ville because they've got some political jive they want to present, and they suspect some Viet Cong are hanging out there tonight.

"You've got orders from this afternoon, so repeat back to me what I want your platoon to do."

Each of the platoon leaders described accurately what he had been told in the helicopter. "Any questions?" I asked.

There were none, and everyone turned to leave.
"Oh, just one more thing," I said. "This is not a practice run."

To relieve the tension, I said, "Thanks for holding me in that bird today. I could have fallen out if you hadn't been so alert." Everyone knew I was teasing them for holding onto me in their moment of fear.

To make sure they understood the seriousness of our operation, I added, "Remember that .50 cal was just a couple villages from our target."

There was laughter and more wisecracks as the platoon leaders went back to their assigned areas. We had some tough work ahead, and we had no way of knowing whether we would engage the enemy before dawn. We had survived this day, in spite of enemy gunners and incompetent pilots, and that was good enough for now.

-Interactive Discussion Guide on Next Page-

Follow the Rules

-Interactive Discussion Guide-

The following questions are intended to stimulate conversation about the story and the noted topic. Participants are encouraged to provide their own experiences and anecdotes to strengthen the discussion.

1. Which character in *Turn Loose* endangered lives and equipment by violating operating rules?

2. What were the consequences of this violation of the rules?

3. Have you experienced casual disregard for established rules? What was the result of their violation?

4. Have the leaders of your organization established an environment in which employees and managers choose to follow the rules?

5. Is there a general attitude of compliance in your organization?

6. What can be done to enhance compliance with established rules and procedures or to implement necessary changes in your organization?

7. With whom will you share these thoughts to help you focus on success and sharpen your ideas?

.

Chapter 9

Is It Worth Doing
A Night in the Graveyard

Older men declare war, but it is the youth who must fight and die.

Herbert Hoover

Is It Worth Doing

In spite of good intentions, it sometimes seems that leaders abandon all logic and issue orders just to confuse the troops. Without apparent reason, changes are needlessly initiated; unnecessary procedures are allowed to continue, and difficult situations are permitted.

Leaders sometimes make poor decisions when they refuse to listen to reason or fail to get advice from subordinates. Other contributing factors are poor communication skills, misunderstanding of the situation, too much stress, lack of self-confidence, and overblown egos.

Every leader needs to make sure the task is worth doing, and they need to be willing to change directions when they find themselves in error.

A Night in the Graveyard

Monsoon rains are amazing when the rain is falling so hard you can't see your hand a few inches in front of your face. Moving about in such a rainstorm is like walking around under water.

People who are native to monsoon territories stay inside if at all possible. Only GIs slog through the rain and mud. I've never seen a single enemy soldier operating in the monsoon rains, nor have I seen high-ranking American officers out there.

The commanders who gave the orders from watertight bunkers also wore dry boots and socks.

When our commander's voice arrived on our radio one tough monsoon afternoon, the RTO had difficulty understanding his words, not because of the weather, but because the caller had a mouth full of food.

While we huddled under poncho tents and sat on our packs in the mud, our leader gave us instructions to move to another location. There was no particular reason to move. No matter how much I tried to believe this move was necessary, it sounded as though we were just going to go sit in the mud on some other rice paddy dike!

The young soldiers were upset by the order. None of them minded such a move if there were reasons for going somewhere, but the expected operation would be completed just in time for us to move out again into a night defensive position. We'd suffer another day without rest, knowing that we had to remain alert all night as well.

The lead elements finally got their stuff together and threw their rucksacks over their shoulders. Almost half an hour passed before the entire company was on the move.

Within a kilometer, we had to cross a river that had jumped its banks, creating a new path through the rice paddy. Evening was approaching by the time we found a way to ford the new river channel, and the rains continued.

Our tactical operations center reported that we were getting four inches of rain per hour, but there was no change in our orders. We were to march toward our objective regardless of the weather or the oncoming darkness.

Our destination was no more than a mark on the map. There were no significant landmarks. Everything was under water, and we were moving along submerged paddy dikes. Every time the paddy dike zigzagged, the point man fell into water up to his chest. Upon pulling him from the water, the next man in the point squad took the lead.

To make sure we didn't lose anyone, we stretched ropes the entire length of the single-file company so our 160 soldiers wouldn't get lost in the dark.

A front to rear headcount was repeated often to make sure we still had everyone. The squad leader in the rear squad radioed up the count to give me a small level of comfort that we had lost no one as the count was passed back from the first man to the last.

Some felt it was impossible to determine our distance or our direction in the daylight, much less at night, but my ranger training had equipped me for contingencies such as this. We were to achieve our objective and meet our commander's requirements, regardless of which movie he watched that night and no matter how difficult the obstacles.

When I checked the time, I found that it was already near midnight. We had at least two more kilometers to go, and I tried to lighten the mood by explaining that we could at least spend the night at the objective.

We would not have to make a second move that night. The remark drew no laughter.

We were barely surviving the operation. A front to rear headcount was often required to make sure we still had everyone. The squad leader in the rear squad radioed up the count to give me a small level of comfort that we had lost no one as the count was passed back from the first man to the last.

GIs continually lost their grip on the rope as they stepped into holes and off the paddy dikes. They quickly scrambled back into their positions, but it would be easy for someone to fall out and not be seen in the darkness.

All noise discipline escaped us. GIs cursed the rain and our rear-area commanders. Our weapons and ammunition were soaked. No longer was the point squad falling into the water—the entire company was moving through waist deep mud and water.

The mortar platoon was especially bitter as they manhandled the heavy mortar tubes and base plates. The weapons were heavy enough in dry weather, but they seemed like boat anchors in this situation.

The heavy machine guns were water-soaked. The machine gunners could no longer hold their weapons above their heads. The ammunition strung around their necks acted as heavy chains, miring them deeper in the mud with each step.

By one o'clock in the morning, the lead squad radioed, "We found some high ground. It's not dry, but it's not under water."

"Make sure there's room for the whole outfit," I answered. "We're only a couple hundred yards from our destination. We'll stop right there if there's room because it's the only thing we've seen above water since we moved out this afternoon."

The entire company crowded onto the muddy rise, which was large enough that we could spread out in a rough circle to protect ourselves against an enemy that would not come out to fight on this particular night.

The radio operator was standing only inches from me when I turned to give instructions about calling our position to the tactical operations center. As I spoke to him in the total darkness, he grabbed my arm and exclaimed surprise as he dropped to my feet. I thought he had collapsed under the weight of his heavy pack and radio, so I lowered myself to my knees, intending to lean over him and ask whether he was injured.

As I leaned over, I found that he was somewhat below ground level. "Captain," he said urgently, "don't move."

"What's happened, Gary?" I said.

"I don't know. I fell into a hole. It's full of water."

"Give me your rifle, Gary. Take my hand, and I'll pull you up."

"OK, but stay back a little. It's really slippery."

We both grunted and groaned and then laid in the mud together as Gary slithered over the edge of the hole.

From another part of our perimeter came a call. "Captain, Captain, come look at this."

"What do you have over there? I'm not moving an inch," I responded.

"One of my guys fell into a hole over here, Captain. It's full of water."

"Well, pull him out. You don't need me."

"We're working on that, Captain. But a tombstone fell in on top of him. He's pinned in the hole."

"Well, get the tombstone off of him, and get him out of the hole. Let me know if he's hurt," I said.

-Stop where you are-

"Gary, tell everybody to stop where they are. We're in a cemetery and these holes you're falling into are the graves."

Gary made the radio call, and the platoon leaders complied. Everyone in the company stopped making an effort to set up a proper defensive position. They all just dropped into the mud and chose up teams for who would stay awake.

Half the GIs pulled ponchos up over their heads and went to sleep with as much water falling on them as there was under them. The other half pulled their ponchos over their heads and tried to stay awake for guard duty.

The morning light awakened me. There was no dawn. There was no rising sun. The total darkness turned to a daylight that was filled with more rain and clouds that seemed to hang just inches above the ground. A headcount confirmed that everyone was still among the living.

Before leaving the cemetery, I walked most of the area to see just how bad our position had been. All around us were gaping holes where graves had collapsed. Tombstones had fallen into the open graves. Large clay burial urns bobbed about like floats on a fishing line in some of the water-filled holes. One GI joked that his life had been saved by a hill full of dead people.

Quick calculations revealed that we were within a few hundred meters of the objective arbitrarily chosen by our commander. We decided to move to the designated grid on the map sheet and call in a situation report.

We could not stop at the objective because it was four feet under water. Most of the day was spent looking for a piece of ground above water level. No one wanted to return to the cemetery.

The rain fell all day long. We eventually found some high ground and decided not to move that night. GIs established a defensible perimeter and tried to heat C-rations beneath hastily erected poncho tents.

The radio operator reported our position to the TOC and set up artillery targets for the night. Those who could stay awake drank coffee or smoked cigarettes before dark. Despite our weariness, there was constant conversation about last night's position.

A few days later, we got a radio call from our civil actions officer (CAO). "What you boys been doing to the cemeteries out there?" he asked.

"We've done nothing to cemeteries except the place we stayed the other night. It was the only piece of dirt we could find above water level. Why do you ask?" I replied.

The CAO quickly explained, "We have a complaint from the local religious leader. He says GIs tore up the graveyard."

My response was a combination of laughter and bitterness as I realized what was going on. "We didn't tear up anything. The monsoon rains caused some graves to collapse. A couple of our GIs fell into the open graves."

The CAO was not phased by my challenging tone. "Well, I'm just telling you what the colonel said. This is just for information because the Army has already paid him several hundred dollars for disturbing the tombs."

Our colonel's persistent moving us around in the monsoon rain had taken a toll on our soldiers. And it cost our taxpayers several hundred dollars. Incidents such as this kept us ever vigilant and somewhat argumentative about orders that seemed illogical.

Is It Worth Doing

-Interactive Discussion Guide-

The following questions are intended to stimulate conversation about the story and the noted topic. Participants are encouraged to provide their own experiences and anecdotes to strengthen the discussion.

1. What alternatives did the company commander have in *A Night in the Graveyard* when he knew the futility of the battalion commander's orders?

2. Explain possible causes for the battalion commander's seemingly inappropriate orders.

3. Describe situations where employees suffered the consequences of inappropriate directives.

4. Are there situations in your organization that need correcting by executive management? What are your alternatives for reporting these situations?

5. In your organization, what are the consequences and alternatives of resisting inappropriate directives?

6. Does your organization have procedures that facilitate reporting these situations? Describe procedures that would help improve situations in your organization.

7. With whom will you share these thoughts to help you focus on success and sharpen your ideas?

-Notes-

Chapter 10

Sense of Humor
A Long War

What people need is a way to
make them smile!

Doobie Brothers

Every American ... lays claim to a "sense" of
humor and guards it as his most significant
spiritual trait, yet rejects humor as a
contaminating element wherever found.

E. B. White

Sense of Humor

Leaders who rule with a heavy club seldom find the respect and reward experienced by those who can see the humor in stressful times.

No matter how serious the situation, there is always room for an understanding remark or a relaxing gesture from key leaders. When times are tough, employees are as stressed as the leaders, and their morale can be accelerated when they see a note of humor in their boss's attitude.

Humor has no place in somber situations. Humor is absolutely offlimits on some occasions, but many stress filled environments have plenty of room for smiles, laughter, and light sarcasm.

Leaders who can laugh at themselves are especially well liked. Their sense of humor generates a reservoir of respect and loyalty that are essential when the going is really tough. If you are a manager who finds it hard to laugh at yourself or your predicament, learn from your subordinates. You can bet they are laughing behind your back.

A Long War

Our days were so filled with activity that I truly thought taking a break in the shade of a banana palm was a luxury. These rest breaks were usually filled with coordinating meetings—in person or by radio—reading reports from the battalion operations center, analyzing maps, coaching platoon leaders, handling disciplinary problems, ordering resupply, or handling administrative matters.

I envied the GIs whose responsibility was simply to carry their weapon and go where they were told. Whenever we stopped for a break, many of these soldiers quickly went to sleep. Only those on guard duty had to remain alert.

The nights were filled with ambush patrols and infrequent enemy contact. The days were filled with reconnaissance patrols. If our company was on operations in the jungle, the company moved as a single unit. But in the flat rice paddies near the coast, we were typically split into squad-sized units except for the mortar platoon. I kept my command group with the mortar platoon since they were not organized or equipped for patrolling in smaller units.

The banana palm was especially inviting on this day because my reports were completed, and I could just take a break like everyone else. My RTO handled the routine communications with our platoons and with battalion headquarters. I had just shaved and cleaned my rifle. I looked forward to rereading some letters from my wife.

-Give me a break!-

When the RTO held the handset toward me, I knew he thought I should take the call. "Gary," I said, "I asked you to screen my calls."

"I screened 'em, Captain. The third platoon says they've got a Viet Cong pack animal out there. They want to know if they can shoot it."

"They're way out to the west," I thought aloud.

"Roger that, Captain. That's where the pack animal is. Out there in the foothills."

"I don't care if they shoot the animal. Tell them to use their best judgment on this."

"OK, if that's what you want," said the radio operator.

Returning to my quest for leisure, I squirted more bug repellent into my hands and rubbed it on my forearms. I was determined to use this break to relax.

"Captain, sorry to bother you again, but the third platoon leader wants to talk to you about that pack animal."

"Did they shoot it?"

"Yes, Sir. They shot it. That's what they want to talk about."

Taking the radio handset, I called third platoon. "Three, this is Six. If y'all shot that pack animal, what else is there to say? Did it attack when you shot it?"

"Six, this is Three. We shot it. It didn't attack, but it crawled off into the bush. Do you think we should follow and make sure it's dead? Over."

"What d'ya mean, crawled off? A water buffalo doesn't crawl. What did you shoot it with? Over."

"We shot it with the machine gun," said the platoon leader. "But this pack animal is no water buffalo."

"Quit talking in riddles. What kind of animal did y'all shoot? Over."

"We found out how the VC have been sneaking all that ammo down from North Vietnam. They've been using big ol' snakes for pack animals, and we found one as big as a telephone pole."

"You mean you shot a giant snake with an M-60?" I asked.

"Roger that, Six. We stitched him right down the side, and he just kept on crawling. We did capture the saddle, though. Do you want us to bring it in, or can we keep it for a souvenir? Over." Before he released his transmitter key, I heard laughter in the background.

Without answering the question, I returned the handset to Gary and said, "What's your bet? Did they really shoot a snake or is the whole thing a joke on me?"

"Now, Captain, do you think I would admit being part of a joke that robbed you of a well-deserved break?" he said.

"I will tell you that they know you hate snakes."

"That's OK," I answered. This is going to be a long war, and I'll have plenty of time to play jokes on third platoon— and on you, my friendly radio operator."

With a big smile, Gary replied, "That's what I like about you, my Captain. You still have a sense of humor."

As I leaned back against the banana palm and closed my eyes, I could hear Gary on the radio. He was taking advantage of his inside knowledge to lightly harass those who had developed the original prank. "I'm not sure what the old man's gonna do. He didn't think your joke was too funny—said something about a long war and how your platoon might need some pack animals where you're going."

-Interactive Discussion Guide on Next Page-

117

Sense of Humor

-Interactive Discussion Guide-

The following questions are intended to stimulate conversation about the story and the noted topic. Participants are encouraged to provide their own experiences and anecdotes to strengthen the discussion.

1. Was it appropriate for the captain in *A Long War* to ask his radio operator to screen his calls?

2. Could the radio operator have handled the prank differently?

3. Will the captain retaliate or continue with the humorous exchange? What makes you think this?

4. Have you experienced managers and leaders who successfully used a sense of humor to their advantage? Site examples.

5. Do you have managers in your organization who apply a sense of humor to the team's advantage? Are there others who seem to have no sense of humor in good times or bad?

6. Are there advantages to working with managers who lack a sense of humor? What alternatives are there for employees whose managers lack a sense of humor?

7. With whom will you share these thoughts to help you focus on success and sharpen your ideas?

Chapter 11

Priorities
Two Boys on a Bike

*Our moral compass should not be
determined by our jobs.*

Dale Collie

Priorities

Conscientious leaders do as well as they can, and their performance depends on their ability at the time, the resources available, and the numerous circumstances that are beyond their control.

After all the decisions are made and operations are under way, every leader needs to keep things in perspective. It is enticing to look back and consider how things might have been done differently, but hindsight, by definition, occurs after the decision-making process is completed.

If you become involved in such retrospectives, you'll find yourself wishing you had made different decisions, treated people differently, and given greater priority to some things in life.

You cannot change any of these things. As you made the decisions and took action, you did the best you could with what you knew. But you can learn from all of these experiences and apply the knowledge in the future.

This is where it is important to keep things in perspective. When events are routine, it is easy to coast through the day without giving importance to the things you rate most highly. When stress abounds, situations become overwhelming, and it is difficult to keep your priorities straight. It helps to visit this subject frequently and ask whether you are keeping things in perspective.

The story about *Two Boys on a Bike* contains numerous examples of how the characters keep things in perspective —and how some of them let their true priorities escape.

As you read this story, reflect on your leadership role. Consider whether you are giving highest priority to the most important things in your life. Consider what the end result will be if you continue the way you are going. Consider whether you need advice on how to get things back into perspective.

Two Boys on a Bike

While everyone stared at me, I exclaimed, "What's going on? What hit us?"

No one said a word, not even the GI who held a bleeding hand.

"What happened to your hand?" I asked.

. . . . .

Soldiers acclimate quickly to the combat environment, whether they are assigned to the rear-area, secure compounds where they get three hots and a cot, or to the frontline units where troops spend weeks and months in the field without a break from full combat alert status.

Those in the rear area suffer from boredom and resent the bureaucratic discipline intended to keep things in control. Many support troops find excitement in fringe activities involving drugs, alcohol, and women, and then find themselves in trouble with their commanders and with their own future.

The life of frontline combat soldiers is entirely different, but soldiers adapt to the hardships and animal-like experience within days.

Even though young Americans readily adapt, daily combat activities have a way of warping a soldier's sense of reality; food from tin cans heated over a small piece of burning plastic explosive; no more than two hours of sleep at a time, day and night; comfort in the dirt if you've dug your foxhole properly; river crossings as a substitute for a bath; never a toilet; never any privacy.

Clean your rifle; patrol through the midday sun; harass a villager; eat beans; and complain about all the stuff you have to carry. Wait until you're told to hurry up. Hurry up and get there so you can wait again. Fight the phantom enemy until the bushes are blown up, and then walk through the rubble to find no enemy at all.

Walk through the rice paddies and then through the jungle. Climb mountains. Cross rivers. Scramble aboard helicopters. Choke for fresh air after breathing tear gas. Vomit a little to get that stuff out of your guts.

Curse the booby trap that wounds your friend. Grab bandages and stop the bleeding—use his, not your own, because you might need to patch your own wounds later in the day. Radio for medivac helicopters when booby traps wound your friends. Toss your buddy onto the chopper and wave a handful of thanks to the anonymous pilots behind their dark glasses.

Curse the enemy. Spoil for a fight. Write a letter home.

Suppress the tears. Refuse to cry. Clean your rifle. Check your grenades. Make sure the safety pin is bent to keep it from falling out. Take off your boots to see if the trench foot has gotten worse. Remove a leach that has made its way into your pant's leg. Tell the guy next to you that the doc has something for that ringworm you see through the skin of his neck.

Trade your cigarettes for the C-ration chocolate bar. Throw away the green eggs and ham and swear that you'll just skip a meal. Run for cover when the sniper bullet snaps past your ear. Roll over and over and over—find cover before he shoots again.

Check the map sheet and take a compass reading to make sure you're going the right way. Stagger under the weight of all that ammo you're carrying.

Day after day the sweat pours from you while you drop iodine tablets into creek water and hope the diseases don't catch up with you. Apply the medic's dope to the cuts made by bamboo grass and pray for a healing of the skin infections.

Brag about the snakes you've seen today, and laugh at anyone who tries to brag about last week's big snakes, or last week's gunfights—they no longer count. We're living for today.

GIs adapted to this life as quickly as a college freshman adapts to his first weeks on campus, and it was from this environment that we took our first break to join those troops in the rear area. Our field troops looked forward to a hot meal with real silverware, a shower, and a cot to sleep on. Some even looked forward to a couple beers and some music.

In reality, we were returning to the secure area to outfit for an extended jungle operation. First we had to make our way back to home base at LZ Bayonet, a part of the military complex at Chu Lai.

-A simple day hike-

Helicopters were always available when rear-area colonels wanted to move us from one bad spot to a worse spot. But choppers were almost never available to move troops from a bad spot to a good spot. We had to walk ten miles across booby-trapped hill country and then through rice paddies and villages to reach the coastal road designated Highway One. It seemed a joke to even give it a number. It was the only highway in that part of Vietnam.

We had orders to rendezvous with trucks for the remaining fifteen miles to the base camp. One hour before pickup, a special truck was to meet us to accept all ammunition, ordinance, explosives, grenades, flares, and anything else that GIs could use to cause trouble in the civilized environment of the support troops.

The soldiers didn't like the idea of turning in all of our weapons, but we did look forward to that ride in the back of the transport trucks. No one needed additional motivation to make the rendezvous point on time.

125

GIs pitched smoke grenades like baseballs. Signal flares and colorful penlight flares made our column look like a parade.

Village children were anxious to get the C-rations tossed by our passing soldiers. Cigarettes were given to the old men of the villages as our company stretched across the countryside. For the first time in weeks, there was an air of levity among these weary teenagers. The promise of a night away from combat miraculously changes the attitudes of soldiers.

To avoid having the entire company inside the roadside village at the rendezvous point, we stopped in the rice paddies just to the west. The lead patrol went forward to make the rendezvous, but we found that we had the typical snafu—the trucks were late.

Radio calls brought us little information about the trucks' arrival time, and the GIs needed some special attention to avoid complications. They had poured out their spare water to avoid having to carry it the last ten miles. They had given away their C-rations and cigarettes.

Platoon leaders had instructions to encourage their men, and patrols were dispatched to avoid surprise by the enemy. Outposts were established nearby.

When I turned to my command group to make sure they were properly informed, one of my RTOs, Jim Cox, noticed that I still had my signal flares and joked that I had not celebrated with the rest of the troops.

Now, a signal flare is nothing more than a one and a half-inch aluminum cylinder filled with fireworks-kind-of-stuff. To fire the flare, you just slip off the tightly fitting cap, place it on the other end, and point the cylinder toward the sky. With your other hand, you slap the cap that strikes the firing pin at the bottom of the tube, and the parachute flare shoots skyward.

I pulled the flare from my rucksack and removed the safety cap to make it ready as a signal to the trucks when they finally arrived in our area, but my plan was overtaken by events of the moment.

-Look out!-

Just as I placed the flare's cap near the bottom of the cylinder, a loud rushing sound overwhelmed us and the six of us hit the ground. The sound was much like that of a Viet Cong rocket, and I knew we were in trouble. I rolled into a ditch and swung my rifle back over the edge of the road to engage the attackers. The men around me did likewise.

But there was no enemy. As a matter of fact, the rest of the company remained standing, looking in our direction. I realized that my perception of events was all wrong, but I didn't know how to reorient myself. Finally, I stood up along with the others.

"What's going on?" I asked. "What hit us?"

All of them stared at me. No one said a word, not even the GI who held a bleeding hand.

"What happened to your hand?"

"The flare got me, Captain."

"What d'ya mean, the flare got you?"

"Your flare went off, Captain. That's what was flying around here."

I stepped into the ditch and picked up the flare to show them that it had *not* been fired, but to my surprise, the tube had been discharged.

"Doc, Doc, come over here!" I shouted to the medic.

"Is anybody else hurt?" I asked the men.

With Doc's arrival, the tension was broken and one young GI started laughing. I was still unsure of just what had happened, but I, too, started to relax. The laughing soldier was pointing to my RTO, Jim Cox, who held his hand against the side of his head.

"Are you hurt, Jim?"

"I don't think so, Captain."

"Why are you holding your head?"

"That flare grazed me. That sucker hit the bamboo and bopped around here like the Fourth of July. I saw it coming off of his hand and jerked my head aside, but it got me anyway."

"I don't see any blood," I said.

"Naw, there ain't no blood," said the laughing GI. "But it gave him a haircut. Look at that. Just as neat as you please."

"Well, Jim, you do look a little better. I've been telling you for days now to cut that hair."

The doc interrupted this banter with, "Captain, I hate to dampen the party, but this guy with a cut hand needs a couple of stitches. He could get by without them, but since we are going to the rear, I'd like to bandage his hand and take him to the hospital when we get back there."

"Roger that, Doc. I feel terrible about this."

"Don't worry about it, Captain," said the injured soldier. "I've been hurt a lot worse than this."

Jim Cox got my attention again and reported a call from the truck convoy that was approaching. "They asked for a signal flare, but I told them we were fresh out."

"That's good, Jim. They'll find the patrol out there on the highway. You're right about the flares, too. I'm not going to take the cap off another one of those flares until I have it pointed skyward. I think static electricity set that thing off because I never got the cap on the bottom of it."

-Surrender your weapons and ammo-

Within an hour, we had all of the weapons and ammo loaded on a special trailer, and the rest of us rode in the back of open two and a half-ton trucks. As the trucks slowed to make their way through traffic, some

129

of the GIs bantered with villagers, and taunts were exchanged. When humorous remarks were taken as insults and tempers flared, it was easy to understand why our commanders required us to secure all weapons before riding through the villages.

As we neared the main compound of Chu Lai, traffic increased. There were more army vehicles on the highway. Civilian trucks carrying produce and people sometimes blocked the way. I passed word back for the GIs to settle down and not talk with the civilians. We didn't have to act like animals just because we lived in the jungle.

Before we reached the base, we came upon the scene of an accident where traffic crept past the tragedy. A truck driven by a South Vietnamese Army sergeant had run over a motor scooter ridden by two young Vietnamese soldiers. They had been dragged beneath the truck, and blood covered the pavement.

I knew that we had been too long in combat when some of our young soldiers made crude remarks and joked about the two dead boys lying on the highway. Others laughed.

As I silently observed the macabre scene, I noticed that some GIs had tears in their eyes. I didn't know whether the tears were caused by the deaths or by their sadness over the remarks of their comrades.

To me, both seemed deserving of tears because those who laughed had been emotionally wounded, perhaps never to recover. I had more hope for those who recognized the sorrow.

The GIs shouted friendly greetings to the MPs as we passed through the gates of LZ Bayonet, and the party-like atmosphere returned. The pace of combat and living-for-today shifted the memory of the accident into the hazy regions of our recollection.

My executive officer and first sergeant welcomed us to the camp. They had worked for days to prepare for our return and re-outfitting. I turned the company over to them for a formation and briefing about times and requirements, knowing that the first thing on their agenda would be hot showers, steak dinners, and cold drinks.

The first thing on my agenda was the resupply, inspection of weapons by the ordinance experts, briefings from the battalion staff about the upcoming operation, and a dozen other very important army things.

-Take care of the troops-

But the most important thing on my agenda was to make special arrangements for the soldier whose hand I had wounded with the flare. Doc got him the proper medical attention, and the first sergeant was charged with finding him a job that would keep him out of the jungles and rice paddies for the rest of his time in Vietnam.

I gave special orders that he was not to be told that we had made these arrangements. He would simply be ordered out of formation the next day as we boarded the helicopters, giving him no opportunity to protest.

On my way to battalion headquarters, I sought out the battalion chaplain who agreed to have a church service for our company the next day. While we awaited the helicopters the next morning, there would be plenty of time for the chaplain to meet with these battle-weary soldiers—before this evening's festivities were overridden by the high drama of another day in combat.

The chaplain was unaware of the traffic accident outside the main gate, so I gave him the news and paused to put things into proper perspective for myself.

"One last thing, Chaplain—say a prayer for the two dead boys and for my troops. All of us are going to need God's help to make it through this war."

-Interactive Discussion Guide on Next Page-

Priterities

-Interactive Discussion Guide-

The following questions are intended to stimulate conversation about the story and the noted topic. Participants are encouraged to provide their own experiences and anecdotes to strengthen the discussion.

1. Give examples of how characters in *Two Boys on a Bike* need to put things into perspective. Explain how their priorities have gone wrong.

2. Identify characters in this story who seem to maintain their priorities in the situations described.

3. Describe situations in your life where different decisions could have been made if you had established the proper priorities. What were the results of confused priorities?

4. Are there situations in your life or your organization that need a different priority?

5. How can you establish priorities for things that need your attention? Would a short-term plan assist in getting started? Would a long-term plan assist in correcting situations one at a time? Where would you start?

6. Who can give you advice on reorganizing priorities in your life or in your organization? Who can assist you with individual elements of your plan?

7. With whom will you share these thoughts to help you focus on success and sharpen your ideas?

Chapter 12

Perseverance
All of These Heroes

Courage and perseverance have a magical talisman, before which difficulties disappear and obstacles vanish into air.

John Quincy Adams (1767 - 1848)

Few things are impossible to diligence and skill. Great works are performed not by strength, but perseverance.

Samuel Johnson (1709 - 1784)

Our greatest glory is not in never falling, but in rising every time we fall.

Confucius

Perseverance

Perseverance—some people have it and some people don't. If you've inherited a good dose of perseverance, consider yourself blessed. If you don't have an ounce of it, let's get to work. You can be just as tenacious, persistent, dogged, and determined as the next person.

You've heard of people with perseverance—Albert Einstein was once told that he had failed ten thousand times in trying to perfect the light bulb, but his own attitude was that he had found ten thousand ways that wouldn't work and that he was one step closer to his goal.

· · · · ·

"Genius is one percent inspiration and ninety-nine percent perspiration." Thomas Alva Edison

· · · · ·

The singer Yanni Chryssomalis (known more popularly simply as Yanni) cannot read music, but he has sold more than ten million albums. It's also reported that famed opera singer Andrea Bocelli cannot read music.

Jack Canfield told me that his book *Chicken Soup for the Soul* was rejected thirty times before it was published. Now, it has sold more than eighty million copies in the USA and has been translated into thirty-five languages.

Military history is filled with stories of success against insurmountable odds because military leaders are taught to persevere. Leaders are not permitted to give excuses; they are expected to succeed. Young leadership cadets are taught that there are only three satisfactory responses—"Yes, Sir," No, Sir," and "No excuse Sir."

Like those in the military, young business leaders need to follow Niki's famous, "Just do it."

I truly don't know whether I gained my perseverance as part of my DNA or whether it was developed through military training. Like you, my family tree shows dozens of ancestors whose perseverance delivered them from tough times in another country and brought them to success in the USA.

The same DNA is in the makeup of those who don't have an ounce of perseverance. So where is the difference?

During my year-long recovery from combat wounds, I found many heroes who couldn't adapt to the recovery. Many of those who seemed to have everything going for them couldn't adapt to changes in their lives and literally took a dive from which they never recovered.

Others who seemed to have insurmountable wounds were able to overcome obstacle after obstacle to gain full recovery. (Read more about this in the chapter on Motivation in *Frontline Leadership* by Dale Collie).

Part of my own recovery involved learning to ski. The instructors took us to the top of the mountain after only an hour or so on the bunny slope. As we looked down the mountain, I remarked that I didn't know how to ski.

The instructor's response was, "You'll know how when you get to the bottom. Just keep getting up and going downhill."

He was right. As an amputee, I learned to ski on one ski, and the sense of accomplishment probably had a big effect on my recovery.

A few years later, I worked with civilians who needed similar recovery, and I was amazed at how many of them simply refused to try. Their constant refrain was, "I can't," much like the soldiers who refused to recover from wounds.

And they were right. If you think you can't, you never will. This is the difference between those who persevere and those who quit. Our goal should be to help people get motivated for success. When they want their goal badly enough, they'll continue in spite of tremendous odds.

All of These Heroes is a first person narrative about my being wounded in combat. The story, however, is about GIs on the frontline of freedom around the world. My story is only intended to illustrate actions in combat and launch you into a discussion about the importance of perseverance in your own organization.

Some say that success is ten percent vision and ninety percent perseverance. What do think?

All of These Heroes

Muted explosions filled my dream. The sound of distant gunfire seemed to ebb and flow. With the louder noises, I sensed that I should awaken, but the dream itself was so real that it held my attention.

Surges of adrenaline called for action, but the dream took priority, luring me back into the comforting darkness of sleep. Slumber fought with wakefulness. Clear thought was elusive. The noise subsided and then returned.

Consciousness approached slowly, bringing an understanding that the battle was no dream at all and that my downy cushion was actually a bed of soft mud.

Suddenly, adrenaline pushed the dream aside and won the battle for my mind. The gunfight was not in the distance; it was all around me.

My eyes popped open.

Tracer rounds passed
just inches above my face.

Machineguns rattled.

There was a lot of rifle fire.

Grenades exploded.

Gun smoke hung in the air.

The smell of battle was strong.

140

A parachute flare lit up the night sky.

Danger was all around.

Caution was dictated by jerky thoughts, slow reactions, and the characteristic sound of live bullets snapping past me.

Holding my head and body perfectly still as I lay there, I moved my arms about, looking for my black gun, the M-16 rifle that had become a part of me during these months of combat. There was no weapon within reach.

Knowing that my life hung in the balance, I pushed the questions aside and quickly rolled to my stomach. Regaining my bearings, I immediately understood where I was. The flare in the sky gave plenty of light, but I couldn't grasp why I was lying on my back in the mud. There was no time to figure it out.

Sluggishly, I thought, "What happened to my rifle? I was just shooting it."

In a split second, the enemy observed my movement and tried to finish me off. All around, miniature geysers of mud leapt into the air as hastily aimed bullets barely missed me.

The only hope for survival was to crawl ten yards forward to hide behind mamma-san's bundled cooking-fire twigs. The gunfire was unrelenting; a near-miss explosion blew mud into my eyes. I had to do something, fast!

-Bullfight-

Just a few hours earlier, our company of infantry had occupied this very same patch of ground and laughed as a water buffalo chased me. In spite of their good humor, this huge beast was dangerous. His well-aimed horns came very close as he tried his best, but his antics seemed no more serious than the barnyard bullfighting games I'd played in my childhood.

Escaping the bovine creature, I laughed with the troops and entertained them with stories from my younger days when I had intentionally taunted bulls to create such a game.

Today's water buffalo needed no taunting, however. He volunteered to play because he was like all the other water buffalos. They hated Americans.

A short time after we left the village, my request for volunteers was met by sharp remarks from one GI.

"I ain't goin back in that ville with the water buffalo, Captain. We might need a recon patrol, but let somebody else go in there."

"Well, this isn't an order," I explained. "I just need a few brave men to help me find out whether a Viet Cong carrying party is in the ville tonight."

The young GI said, "Count me out. I don't mind them VC, but somebody told me that water buffalo sleep standing up, and I don't need none of that."

Within moments Lieutenant John (Harvey) Frey and my radio operator volunteered. A few more GIs signed on, and the patrol was formed.

"What I'd like to do is sneak into the middle of the ville and see who's picking up all that rice we found when the buffalo attacked me. You saw how they had it hidden. I expect a carrying party will pick it up tonight, before we can send in helicopters to remove the cache."

Lieutenant Frey asked, "What are we going to do if we find Charlie in the ville, Captain?"

"We're just going to watch," I said. If we find them carrying off that rice, we'll let our ambush patrols do the heavy work outside the village.

"OK," I continued, "here's how we'll run this patrol. We'll leave all our gear here at the command post. Take only your weapons and ammo. Gary, you bring the radio. About a half hour before dark, report back here with your night camouflage on. Tape down anything that will make noise. I'll inspect your gear and go over our exact route before we move out."

Just before nightfall the team reassembled, and we went through the drill once again. Everyone knew the village and the landmarks. Rally points were designated and details were coordinated.

Two of our line platoons left the perimeter to establish ambush sites surrounding the village. The third infantry platoon moved to a designated position to help our patrol if we got into trouble, and the mortar platoon established a temporary position that would be abandoned after our patrol returned from the village.

-Time to go-

These night patrols were routine to our troops, so there was no anxiety leading up to our departure. This was just another night's work.

"RTO," I said, "tell the TOC we're on the move. It's time to go." The troops sitting on the ground quietly stood and turned to leave the perimeter.

"Roger," he responded as the point man moved in the direction of the village.[2]

. . . . .

Heavy afternoon rains had soaked the grass and weeds. We could move with absolute silence. Not a word was spoken, and self-imposed radio silence precluded any transmissions as we covered the distance to the village.

In the darkness we followed each other single file and approached the village from the west. We were upwind and a good distance from the buffalo corral. No one wanted to stir up those animals again.

At the edge of the ville, we paused and quietly got down on our hands and knees to crawl the remaining hundred yards into the center of town. Only the

---

[2] A likeness of this image can be seen in the bronze statues standing near the Vietnam memorial in Washington, D.C. The artist has captured the look and feeling of soldiers moving out on patrol at twilight.

sensitive nose of a dog or water buffalo could give us away, but the gentle breeze off the South China Sea remained in our favor.

The seriousness of the effort quickly drove away fleeting recollections of cowboy and Indian movies that told of patrols sneaking undetected into the middle of enemy encampments. Total concentration brought to mind the training I'd had for such missions.

The point man paused and sat on his heels as I crawled up next to him. Cupping his hands to contain the lightest of whispers, he spoke directly into my ear, "Somebody just walked right in front of me."
"Keep going another twenty yards," I whispered back to him. The crawl continued.

We knew this village, and we had practiced for such a patrol. It was no surprise that we easily found the exact spot we wanted and spread out to observe the enemy.

-Not a good plan-

Using an unspoken, prearranged signal, the radio operator silently directed artillery to fire a parachute flare high above us to illuminate the darkness. We thought we had our positions established, but during the flare's inbound flight, I made one final move to give me a better view of what was going on.

Half crouching and half standing, I stepped toward a banana palm that would conceal me as I observed the village.

145

Before I reached the tree, the flare lit up the sky like Miami Beach at high noon.

-What to do-

The flare ignited a trained response that required my body to freeze in place. If this had been a ground flare, I would have run out of the illuminated zone as fast as I could.

However, aerial flares cast light over such a broad expanse, it is impossible to run without attracting enemy attention. The strategy for this situation required that I drop to the ground or freeze in place, depending upon the amount of light, the presence of the enemy, and so on.

I froze. But my training wasn't the only reason I froze in place.

Standing directly in front of me, not ten feet away, was an enemy soldier, right there on the front porch of a grass hut! If he had been dressed in the VC's familiar black pajama uniform, my trigger finger would have reacted on its own to fire the rifle I held loosely at waist level.

But this man was not dressed for combat. He wore khaki trousers and a brilliant white shirt. His shoes were highly shined, as was the leather belt that crossed his chest from left to right and circled his waist. On his shoulders were officer's epaulets. And his right hand held the business end of a Russian-made AK-47 rifle that stood on the ground by his right foot.

Just as I was caught unaware by his presence, he was totally surprised by my standing before him in my blackened and camouflaged, mud-covered combat uniform.

Time seemed to stand still as my mind raced through the alternatives. In spite of all my training and months of combat experience, confusion held the moment while I considered whether I should shoot him.

Instantly, he lifted the rifle that stood by his side, and I thought, "This could be a national police officer, but they said they wouldn't be in this village tonight."

. . . . .

Valuable time escaped as an irritating random thought recalled movie scenes of cowboys facing each other on the dusty streets of the Old West and drawing their six-shooters. The famed gunfight at the OK Corral came to mind, but the enemy across from me was drawing his own gun. There was no time to think about cowboy movies.

. . . .

As his left hand grabbed the center of his rifle, I thought, "He's not a national policeman, not even a South Vietnamese Army officer, because both said they wouldn't be here tonight."

. . . . .

Now, holding the rifle with his left hand, the man seemed to be in slow motion as he moved his right hand from the barrel tip to the trigger guard. My analysis continued as I wondered, "Could this be a US Marine? They operate here from time to time, but even marines wouldn't wear dress uniforms into the villages at night!"

. . . . .

I could see fear in the officer's very wide eyes, and I knew that this man was more than just an enemy soldier. With just a few feet between us, and only a fraction of a second to understand all there was to know, I realized that this was someone's son, probably someone's husband, and a father of young children.

. . . . .

Was he thinking the same thing about me? Did my eyes reflect my thoughts? I didn't want to shoot. Wasn't there some way we could just relax these weapons of war?

. . . . .

Instead, we were both overcome by events. Just as my presence required him to shoot in self-defense, the downward swing of his rifle barrel required me to pull the trigger. Reactions finally kicked in. Without a conscious thought to do so, my trigger finger did its work.

My rifle barrel was forced upward as twenty bullets left my weapon. My left hand expected the rise and automatically knew how to hold the weapon down. The rapid fire pushed the rifle butt back along my belt line, but my right elbow also knew what to expect and pressed in tightly to direct the weapon.

These things I remember clearly—and then the dream.

-It's not all mud-

As I regained consciousness and realized that I must seek cover behind mamma-san's cooking twigs, I knew that bad things had happened. I just didn't know the details. There was no time to sort it out.

Bullets plowed into the mud all around me. If one of them found its mark, there would be no need for the twigs or anything else. When a bullet blew a small geyser of mud into my face, I started crawling.

Progress was very slow. Plenty of low-crawl training had prepared me for this effort, but I wasn't covering the ground that I should.

· · · · ·

My mind raced with ridiculous thoughts. "When I get back to the States, I'm going to write the commanding general and explain that these uniform buttons are just too large. They're keeping me too high off the ground, and they're slowing me down."

· · · · ·

My left leg wasn't giving me the push it should, but there was no pain. There was no fear—just a realization that bullets were all around me. The sticks were a few feet away.

When I reached the bundled twigs, time resumed its normal pace. With my head and shoulders behind the sticks, I was almost hidden from enemy eyes, but the tender twigs provided no protection. Bullets cracked through them, adding the snap of the twigs to the usual snap of passing bullets.[3]

---

[3] Years after I returned from combat, one of my sons sneaked behind me to flick my ear with his fingers. He missed my ear,

Just when the sticks hid me, I felt the searing pain of a bullet just above my ear. The impact of the bullet was stunning, but not nearly as painful as the blow when my head hit the ground.

I laid perfectly still and prayed that the enemy would think I was dead.

The gunfire was momentarily surreal.

The parachute flare was still up there.

The battle continued.

The crawl had exhausted me. I needed rest. Gasps for breath brought little relief. Something foul covered my face and clogged my nose.

I quickly recognized the smell. This morning's combative water buffalo had cushioned the blow to my head with a well-positioned cow pie. Now, blood covered one side of my face and buffalo pie covered the other.

Things seemed bad, but the worst was yet to come.

-Are you OK?-

To the radio operator I called, "Gary, are you OK?"

---

and I surprised both of us by diving to the floor. My heart slowed as he explained what he had done. We laughed together at that event and many times afterwards, whenever he found me so focused on my work that he could imitate the sound of passing bullets with only a flick of a finger very near my ear.

"I'm OK," he yelled back through the sound of gunfire. "I'm over here behind the hooch. Are you OK?" he asked.

"I think I'm wounded, but I can't look right now. Is the radio working?"

"It's working. Whatcha want me to do?"

"Call Red Leg and turn off the lights," I commanded. And in rapid succession he followed this command and others as I gave orders.

"Call for a medivac. Call for Cobra gun ships, and tell the reserve we're pinned down. Tell them to come here now, running and screaming down the trail so Charlie will know they're coming in."

In the midst of his calls, Gary let me know he would take care of these things, and we started to see results.

When the last flare expired, it was dark again. Our night vision was ruined, and the barrel flash of continuing rifle fire was the only thing we could see.

Gary yelled back to me, "Medivac's on the way. Cobras have lifted off. Reserve's coming in."

The gunfight intensified and subsided as we heard the nearby reserve shouting loudly on their way toward us. Guided by the ongoing fight, the platoon ran right into the middle of the village.

A young Puerto Rican soldier rolled onto his stomach right beside me. He had no way of knowing that I was his company commander when he asked, "How you doing?"

"I don't know. Check my leg and tell me what you see."

"Hey, you're hit real bad. You've got bones sticking out through your pant's leg."

"I'll work on the leg. Stop Charlie from shooting at us. Do you see him?"

"I can see his gunshots."

"Shoot him. I've lost my rifle."

"We're too close. I've got this grenade launcher, and the grenade won't arm itself in that short distance."

"It doesn't matter," I said. "If you even get close to him with one of those baseballs, he's going to quit shooting at us."

Sticking his weapon around the end of the twigs, the GI fired at the unseen enemy. We received no more fire from his direction.

While the GI continued the fight, I pulled off my belt and sat behind the sticks to tie a tourniquet on my left leg. The village filled with hollering GIs. Just as I had hoped, the VC could hear the cavalry coming to our rescue.

-Medivac-

As Charlie broke off the fight and headed for the hills, we discovered two more wounded GIs. A rifleman was wounded in the leg, and Lieutenant John Frey was wounded in the chest.

"Roll him over and use that aluminum foil pack to cover the exit wound," I ordered in the darkness.

"We already did that. We've covered the wounds front and back. We're applying pressure in both places. Where's that medivac?"

"Ten minutes out," responded the RTO.

"The leader of the reserve platoon was nearby when I told him, "You're in charge of the company now. Set up a perimeter here and in that clearing to the west. We'll land the medivac over there."
"Roger that," he answered.

Quickly taking charge, he told second platoon, "Take the LZ. I'll set up here and make sure we don't have any VC left in our perimeter."

While the RTO worked the radio, our largest GI, nicknamed Tiny, grabbed from the roof of a hut a piece of tin to use as a litter. The tin was nailed down, but his strength and adrenalin enabled him to pull it free with small effort.

Lieutenant Frey was quickly moved to the clearing. The other wounded GI was carried out next; then, without delay, Tiny returned with the litter and asked, "Are you ready to go, Captain? The other two are at the LZ."

When Tiny and his partners lifted me onto the litter and headed up a small incline, the GI by my side stumbled and lost his grip on a corner of the tin roofing. The action jerked the tin from another GI's hand, and I rolled down a small slope.

"Oops," said Tiny.

"Take your time," I groaned. "I don't hear the medivac yet."

The radio operator responded by saying, "They say they're right on top of us and want us to shine some flashlights."

"Well, tell them they're not anywhere close. Give them our grid in the open and tell them to recheck everything."
"Roger" was his simple reply.

Tiny took charge of the LZ, and when we heard the sound of helicopters nearby, he turned on a number of flashlights to guide them. After several minutes of confusion, he discovered that the choppers were actually Cobra gun ships, not the medivac helicopter.

Gary coordinated between the Cobras, the medivac, and the TOC and finally directed the rescue choppers to our LZ.[4]

---

[4] Gary Salpini was an excellent soldier and radio operator. He expertly handled the breakout of our patrol when we were pinned down in the village. Afterward, he accomplished the impossible by directing the misplaced medivac choppers to our LZ. Gary was awarded the Silver Star, the Army's second highest medal of valor, for his work in the village and during the rescue.

The flashlights were ineffective by the time the medivac finally arrived. Gary recommended using a flare to mark our spot on the ground, reminding us about Jim Cox's haircut and the misfired flare we had experienced weeks before (p. 128 in Chapter 11).

Everyone was warned about the plan, and the flare ricocheted off the bamboo around the clearing before landing exactly in the middle. It could not have been planned better.

The wounded rifleman was put aboard first, and then I was lifted into the arms of two medics crouched in the doorway of the helicopter. The engine rotation accelerated, and we began our ascent.

"Hey, put LT on the chopper!"

"He's dead. We can't fly the dead with the wounded," I was told, and a series of fragmented thoughts flooded my mind.

· · · · ·

Harvey Frey needed a lot of medical help, fast—more than our field medics could give him. He couldn't be dead. We had to get him to the hospital quick!

· · · · ·

Following our medivac, he essentially commanded the company by advising the acting company commander appointed as my replacement until the arrival of another captain the next morning, assembling the unit, guiding their movement to a safer location, and setting up a night defensive position several kilometers away.

Even if he were dead, our company would have to leave this position and set up somewhere else before Charlie came back to strike again. I sure didn't like the idea of our troops carrying Lieutenant Frey through the night.

. . . . .

The enemy always fired at rescue medivacs. Charlie didn't buy into the Geneva Accord that prevented shooting at clearly marked medical vehicles. They would surely fire at this one if we landed again, and I had witnessed the fiery result of helicopters plowing into the ground (*Frontline Leadership,* Chapter 2— "Death in the Afternoon").

. . . . .

For the first time in the war, I felt fear myself. If we went back for LT, we could all die in a ball of fire.

. . . . .

"LT's not dead," I yelled. "Set the chopper down!"
The engine continued its whine, and we continued to climb.

"Go back! Go back! He's not dead! Go back!" I ordered, over and over again.

The pilot listened to my plea, and we began our descent. With every passing second, I waited for the sound of bullets striking the helicopter. The skids briefly touched down, and the other wounded GI and I helped pull Lieutenant Frey aboard.

Finally free to leave the LZ, the brave night-flying pilot took us up to ten thousand feet for the forty-five-minute flight to the emergency hospital at Chu Lai.

Deliveries like ours were routine at the MASH hospital, and the helicopter landed on the dimly lit tarmac, just far enough from the emergency entry to avoid endangering personnel but close enough to permit transfer of wounded GIs by gurney.

-Buffalo pie?-

Doctors and nurses treated each of us in separate rooms as I asked, "How about those other two GIs? Did they make it OK?"

The question went unanswered as they cut my uniform away.

"Did anyone give you morphine yet?" asked one of the doctors.

"No. Can you give me a shot now?"

"Are you in pain?" asked a nurse who was cleaning my head wound.

"No. But big pain is coming when you remove that tourniquet," I answered.

"Who put the tourniquet on?" responded the doctor, again avoiding my question about morphine.

"I put it on—in the middle of a gunfight."

"How'd you do that and shoot at Charlie?"

"I wasn't doing any shooting. When I got hit the first time, it knocked me out. I don't know how long I was out, but when I came to, I had no rifle. I don't know what happened to it."

157

"Did you get the head wound at the same time?" asked the nurse by my side.

"No. That came later."

"I'm going to shave your hair to treat this wound. First, I have to wash your head. What is this stinking stuff?"

"Smells like buffalo pie," I said.

As I explained what happened, the staff laughed so much that they had to stop working on me. The lead doctor laughed so hard, he put one hand on the shoulder of a second physician and held his own stomach with the other hand.

"Hey, you guys quit laughing and get back to work. I'm not here for entertainment," I joked.

"We apologize, Captain, but this is the first time we've laughed in days. I actually thought we'd forgotten how to laugh."

Everyone was having such a good time over my predicament, I joined in the humor of the moment and drew another round of laughter with a description of that morning's bullfight.

The nurse at my head knew the pain was just minutes away and spoke about the morphine I'd requested. "We'll give you a shot as soon as we find out whether you have a concussion. In the meantime, let us know when the pain arrives. You're in shock and that might be holding the pain back. When it comes, it will be fast.

"Now, relax while I give your dirty little head a wash and the doc works on that leg wound."

Oblivion took over as I relaxed into their care, and several days passed before I awoke on a medical ward with twenty other wounded soldiers.

There was no transition to wakefulness as I'd experienced lying in the mud near that grass hooch. One moment I was unconscious, and the next moment my eyes were wide open. My first impression was of the clean white sheets and the contrast between this bed and the jungle growth and rice paddy mud where I'd slept for the preceding six months.

"How long have I been here?" I asked the soldier on my left. He stared right at me but didn't answer.

When I rolled my head to the right, the soldier in that bed explained, "You were here when they brought me in three days ago. I've got a stomach wound," he mumbled. "Are you OK?"

"I don't know. Have they said anything about this cast on my leg?"

"Nope. Did you hear me say I've got this stomach wound?

"Look at all my tubes," he said through the gear hanging around his face. "They check on you all the time—wish they checked on me that much. Stomach wounds are bad. I got shot in the stomach.

"You got shot in the head," he continued. "I can tell by those bandages."

I made a move to touch my head, but found both wrists tied to the bed frame.

In response to my puzzled look, the soldier explained, "They tied your hands down so you wouldn't accidentally pull out those IV needles. See here, I've got the same thing, but I ain't tied down.

"Unless you're one of the wild ones, they'll probably untie your hands when you regain consciousness. See that old boy over there? They had to dope him up with something because he tried pulling out his tubes when he came out of his coma."

A passing nurse heard us talking and exclaimed, "Hey there soldier boy! You're finally awake. I'm glad you're going to make it."

"What do you mean, make it?" I asked.

"Well, you know, make it. You're going to survive and get well," she said, with a mixture of joy and embarrassment at letting me know she had worried about my survival.

"Was there some question about that?" I asked.

"Well, don't you even think about that, soldier boy. I'm going to tell the doc that you're awake. It's going to make him real happy."

160

The doctor arrived within minutes and expressed his pleasure about my impending recovery. "Both bones were shattered above your ankle," he explained. "That bullet also cut the artery, but we patched it. To tell you the truth, you're doing pretty well for losing so much blood. You need to thank the guy who put that tourniquet on your leg. Without it, you would have bled to death before they got you back here."

"When do you think you'll amputate my leg, Doc?"

"What makes you think you're going to lose the leg, Captain?"

"When they taught me about tourniquets, they taught me about gangrene. Those black toes sticking out of my cast sure look like gangrene."

"That's not gangrene. It's typical of severed arteries. I think you're going to be OK."

"Doc, severed arteries is what makes gangrene. Either those guys who taught me about gangrene were lying, or you're making a bad mistake. I'm interested in having my leg amputated before that gangrene goes all the way up my leg."

"Look. You just woke up from a few days' sleep. We'll pay attention to that leg. Just rest, and I'll come back to see you in awhile. You're going to be just fine now."

"OK, Doc, but if that smell gets any stronger, I hope you'll open up this blood covered cast to see what's going on in there."

"Don't worry, Captain. You rest now. You'll be going to the States soon." The nurse adjusted the IV drip, and my focus faded rapidly.

-Last rites-

Mumbling about "looking forward to that stateside ride," I fell asleep again. There were no dreams—just plenty of long-needed rest.

My eyes were still closed when I heard a voice happily announce, "Oh, I'm glad you're awake."

"What day is this?" I asked, opening one eye against the bright light of midday.

"December 8th. When did you come in here?" he asked.

"I think it was December 3rd, at night," I replied.
There must have been a question in my eyes, because he responded with, "Of course it was December 3rd. I just asked to see whether you're fully conscious. I came to see you the night you got wounded, and I came back today to thank you for getting Lieutenant Frey aboard that helicopter."

As my visitor leaned over my bed to make these remarks, I recognized the chaplain's insignia sewn to his collar.

"How's LT doing, Chaplain? Was that chest wound pretty bad?"

"I'm sorry to be the one to break the news, Captain. I thought you already knew that he didn't make it. But

I'm thankful that you brought him back with you. He lived for awhile, and I was able to give his last rites."

"Oh," I said, and turned to face the other direction, where my eyes met those of another wounded soldier just a few feet away, a different soldier than the last time I awakened.

The new patient said, "Hi," and I ignored his remark as I thought about the death of Lieutenant Frey and his family in Louisiana. He was married just before coming to Vietnam. Did he tell me his wife was pregnant? Had his family been notified? Confusion took over amidst the drugs and the emotional pain was greater than the physical pain.

After awhile, I turned back toward the chaplain, but he was gone. Pinned to my pillow case was a "Purple Heart" medal, evidently from an earlier visitor.

The patient on my right said, "Hi," and I ignored the greeting.

"Another new guy," I thought.

Consciousness came and went over the next several days. The narcotic administered for my pain was doing its job, but it also altered reality.

-Phone calls-

There was plenty of pain, intermittently relieved by drugs, and the one hundred twenty-degree heat found its way through the ever-slamming screen door and past the ineffective ceiling fans. The medical staff was the same each time I awakened, but the patients seemed to change constantly.

Broken bones, burns, cuts, bullet wounds, grenade fragments, eye coverings, bandages, and the smell of medicine. Some soldiers screamed in pain. Others stared glassy-eyed. Some joked, and we laughed through the pain. Casts. Crutches. IV stands and gurneys. Food trays. Water bottles. Bed pans. And tubes—lots of tubes.

With joyful but confusing remarks, a medic interrupted this bizarre scene and plugged a phone into the wall near my bed. He said, "It's your wife."

"Bad joke," I thought. But Char was on the phone, having received a hand-delivered Western Union telegram. It's surprising how she tracked me down in the middle of Vietnam, getting a call through the various military channels to connect with my hospital bed. But the sound of her voice truly gave me new inspiration and got me focused on recovery.

The same medic came on another occasion and announced that my mother was on the phone. The connections for both calls were very sketchy, with a time lag between each of our remarks. Considering the state of telephone technology and the bureaucratic maze of military communication, these calls were about as miraculous as my own survival.

-You're going to be OK-

"Hey, have I met you before?" I asked a GI in the bed next to me when I awakened one afternoon.

"Nope. I just came in this morning. Stepped on a punji stake. Went in the side of my boot and right through my ankle. They said I'll heal pretty fast, but I'm on my way to the States. How about you?" he asked. "Are you hurt bad?"

164

Instead of answering his question, I asked, "Were you here when they put this new cast on my leg?"

"Yep. I was here. We were all talking about you when they wheeled you out. Some thought you were dead, but then they brought you back, and we had to admit we were wrong." He laughed as though I was supposed to join him in his attempt at being funny.

"So, did you hear the medics talking about amputation or anything like that?"

"Nope. They just said you were going to make it."

"Well, thanks, but I've been trying to get them to amputate for quite awhile. What day is it, anyway?"

"I don't know," he said. "Hey, over there with the newspaper—what day is it?"

"It's the 18th," said the young soldier with one arm in a cast. Two weeks had passed, and I was certain that I would lose my leg. The only question in my drug-fogged mind was how far up they would amputate.

Within a few days I was transferred to another hospital in Vietnam and assured, once again, that amputation was unnecessary.

When I was shipped to Camp Zama, Japan, a couple of days later, the receiving triage doctors agreed with my own diagnosis. "Take him to surgery. Mark it on his chart and call ahead—amputation left leg."

The medic pushing my gurney was well-practiced in navigating the hallways. He filled the air with small talk about highly skilled surgeons and such. Before going into the operating theater, we coasted to a stop along one wall, where he told me that many soldiers were doing well with artificial legs. He was trying to console me, so he was taken completely off guard when I interrupted his woeful explanation.

"Buddy, you don't know how glad I am that someone has finally agreed to take off this leg. I've been telling them that it's gangrene! I'll see you when surgery is over."

As he pushed me through the swinging doors, I reached out and shook his hand, saying, "Thanks for your help. It means a lot."

For me, going into surgery was good news because I was finally getting some action on the gangrene that had concerned me since the day I came out of my initial coma. Coming out of the recovery room after surgery, however, I felt quite the opposite.

A helicopter passing just over the hospital wing triggered in me an emotional response and an exaggerated concern for the GIs I'd left behind.

"Nurse, wait awhile before going into the ward," I pleaded through my tears.

"I have to get back to my company. Those guys need me," I sobbed. "Who's going to take care of them? Who's going to take care of them?"

"They have a new company commander now," she explained. "They're going to be OK. You're going to be OK."

She pushed me right into the ward, where my crying attracted no attention at all. Her remark, "You're going to be OK," became a mantra echoed by all the medical staff.

Before long, I learned that while these dedicated, war-weary people truly intended the phrase for the patients, it was also a way for them to reassure themselves as they cared for the young broken bodies headed back for the USA.

After many years of survivor's guilt about the loss of Lieutenant Frey and thinking all the while that I had killed the officer in the brilliant white shirt, God blessed me with a realization that I never actually knew what happened to the Vietnamese soldier whose wide eyes looked into mine as we fired our weapons at each other. I don't even know if my bullets found their mark.

It is possible that someone else wounded me that night, or maybe the officer I faced simply outgunned me while my mind searched for reasons not to shoot. Maybe he is now telling grandchildren about the night an American soldier appeared from the darkness and started shooting.

Certainly, I could have made different decisions that would not have endangered the young lieutenant. Hindsight shows me many, many alternatives. All I know for sure is that I did the best I could with what I knew.

The night was filled with tragedy, but it was also filled with heroes. Every GI who came to rescue our patrol in the face of danger deserves a medal of valor. Those who flew the choppers demonstrated bravery beyond the call of duty. And the medical staffs of all military hospitals deserve recognition for patching the wounded and helping the dying.

There should be great respect for those in our military who sacrifice their lives, and not to be forgotten are the surviving families of these brave Americans, where the pain lives on and the war is never entirely over.[5]

All of these heroes deserve our admiration and appreciation as our nation protects freedom-loving people around the world. Wherever you encounter veterans or families who gave their brave sons and daughters, thank them for their efforts because they've all confronted danger and faced the crises that belong to all of us.[6]

-Interactive Discussion Guide on Next Page-

---

[5] Thirty years after this fateful night, I received an e-mail from a friend of Lt. Frey, asking whether I knew anyone who could tell him how his college buddy had died. I sent him a book, which he later passed to someone in Lt. Frey's family. This friend had contacted the only person in the world who could give him answers to his decades-old questions.

[6] Lt. John Harvey Frey represents all of those who have given their lives for freedom. The troops who fought their way into the village to rescue the patrol and the helicopter pilots represent brave soldiers around the world who care enough for others to endanger themselves. My own role in this story is one that represents all of those who spend their post-combat lives recovering from the trauma. The friends and family of Lt. Frey and all the other soldiers represent what it takes for an army to win a war—a courageous and supportive home front. These are the heroes.

Perseverance

-Interactive Discussion Guide-

The following questions are intended to stimulate conversation about the story and the noted topic. Participants are encouraged to provide their own experiences and anecdotes to strengthen the discussion.

1. Give examples of perseverance in *All of These Heroes* (doing what needs to be done, no matter how difficult).

2. Identify characters in this story who seemed to persevere. How did they persevere?

3. Describe situations in our life where perseverance has made a difference. What were the results of your efforts?

4. Are there situations in your life or your organization where perseverance would make a difference?

5. How can people learn to persevere?

6. Would perseverance make a difference in your management team? How could your leaders encourage perseverance? Examples.

7. With whom will you share these thoughts to help you focus on success and sharpen your ideas?

—GLOSSARY—

The terms and phrases in this glossary are intended for readers who have little or no exposure to military technical terms and jargon. They are not textbook definitions.

- GLOSSARY -

.45 – US Army standard issue .45 caliber pistol.

Ammo – Ammunition.

Army Units –

Brigade – An infantry brigade consists of the brigade commander, a brigade staff, and three or more battalions and other support units as required by the assigned mission.

Battalion – An infantry battalion consists of the battalion commander and his staff, along with three or four frontline companies and a headquarters company.

Company – An infantry company consists of a company commander, executive officer, first sergeant, and four platoons of forty-four soldiers.

Platoon – An infantry platoon consists of a lieutenant platoon leader and four squads of eleven soldiers each. Sergeants are sometimes assigned as platoon leaders in combat.

Squad – Infantry squads consist of eleven soldiers, and there are four squads in a platoon.

Arty – Artillery.

Dink – Slang for enemy soldier.

Deuce and a half – 2.5-ton army truck.

Battalion – *See Army Units.*

Big Six – Slang for *battalion commander*, derived from the radio call sign that typically included the word *six* to refer to a commanding officer.

Bird – Slang for *helicopter*.

Break squelch – Key the radio handset to *break* the rushing noise, or *squelch*, heard when no one is transmitting on that frequency. This procedure was often used to signal others when the nearness of enemy soldiers made the sender reluctant to speak into the handset. Because most radio transmissions were uncoded, soldiers would sometimes *break squelch* to keep the enemy from understanding the intended signal; for example, a platoon leader might *break squelch* three times to tell the company commander that his unit was in place and ready to attack.

Brigade – *See Army Units.*

Blue Six – Military personnel who are assigned communications radios are also given a radio call sign. Call signs are changed frequently in an effort to prevent enemy intelligence gathering activities. In this case, the word *blue* was the word that would be changed. The word *six* indicated the call sign given to the unit commander. *Six Alpha* was the designation of the radio operator working with *six*.

Captain – See *US Army Officer Ranks.*

Charlie – Army slang for *Viet Cong* (VC) *soldiers*, derived from the US Army phonetic alphabet used in radio transmissions. The abbreviation VC would be communicated as Victor Charlie by radio to ensure correct understanding of the individual letters, ergo the shorter reference to Charlie.

Chopper – Slang for *helicopter*.

Chu Lai – A very large US Army, US Navy, and US Air Force compound approximately one hundred miles south of Da Nang, Vietnam. Population and acreage of this logistical center was similar to a medium-size U.S. city with its own airport.

CO – Commanding officer (or *conscientious objector*, as my wife discovered while aboard an airplane on her way to join me in Germany. When the woman beside her explained that her husband was a CO, a period of confusion ensued while they figured out that this acronym had more than one meaning. Her husband was a conscientious objector, avoiding the draft, while I was a commanding officer, leading mechanized infantry troops on the border of Germany and the Czech Republic).

Colonel – *See US Army Officer Ranks.*

Company – *See Army Units.*

Court martial – Slang for the *court martial procedure* and punishment used by the military in lieu of the civilian procedure of courts, judges, and punishment.

C-rations – Precooked, canned meals.

ETA – Estimated time of arrival.

Fatigues – Olive drab US Army combat uniform for labor or for field duty in the 1960s, prior to the introduction of today's camouflage uniforms, which have been renamed BDUs—Battle Dress Uniforms.

First Lieutenant – *See US Army Officer Ranks.*

Free fire zone – An area where there is no requirement to obtain permission before firing at a suspected enemy target.

Firefight – Gunfight.

Full oughta get-'em – The M-16 rifle carried by American soldiers has a safety switch that can be set to single shot or full automatic. This slang phrase was used in reference to the full automatic position on the selector switch.

GI – Slang for *soldier*, derived from the term *government issue.*

Grid – Slang for *map location.* The numbered horizontal and vertical lines that crisscross all military maps are known as *grid lines.* The purpose of these lines is to aid in identifying specific locations.

Grunt – Slang for US Army infantryman.

Gunship – An armed aircraft, such as a helicopter, that is used to support troops and provide fire cover.

Hammer and anvil operation – A tactical maneuver that positions one unit as a blocking force and uses other units to encircle the enemy and drive them into the blocking force with the intention of trapping them, hammering them from both front and rear.

Hooch – Slang for *huts* constructed of bamboo and thatch

Jungle penetrator – A device mounted on selective helicopters, consisting of cables and pulleys that lower a seat through jungle canopy to rescue wounded soldiers from areas where helicopters cannot land.

KP – Kitchen Police, those soldiers assigned temporarily to help clean up, or *police*, the kitchen.

Landing Zone (LZ) – Permanent landing zones at established base camps (e.g., Landing Zone Bayonet)

as well as impromptu landing zones established by frontline troops.

Lieutenant – *See US Army Officer Ranks.*

Lieutenant Colonel – *See US Army Officer Ranks.*

Lima Charlie – Army slang for *loud and clear*, derived from the US Army phonetic alphabet used in radio transmissions.

LT – Slang for "lieutenant," the rank of most platoon leaders. *See US Army Officer Ranks.*

LZ – *See Landing Zone.*

M-16 – The standard rifle carried by the US Army infantry during and after the late 1960s.

Major – *See US Army Officer Ranks.*

Medivac – Medical evacuation, usually by helicopter.

Mortars – Mortars are tube-like weapons that are secured to baseplates for firing. The baseplates are placed on the ground to support the vertical tube. Ammunition consists of the round itself and multiple packets of *charges* (somewhat like gunpowder). To fire the weapon, the properly charged round is dropped down the tube, where it strikes a firing pin that ignites the *charge*, propelling the round skyward. The proper positioning of the tube aims the round so it will arc through the sky and land on its target. A mortar platoon consists of three such mortars and soldiers to calculate just how to aim the mortars and load the *charges*.

Newbies – Newly assigned soldiers.

NVA – North Vietnamese Army.

OCS – Officer Candidate School.

Operations Officer (S-3) – At battalion level, the operations officer is the person designated to draft plans for training, operations, and combat. Battalion commanders rely on these highly trusted, capable officers to plan and manage operations at all levels. This position at battalion level is referred to as S-3 (staff officer #3).

Ops Officer – *See Operations Officer.*

Peter Principle—The practice of promoting people to their level of incompetence – *promote them until they fail.*

Platoon –*See Army Units.*

Pop smoke – Ignite a smoke grenade, usually to signal an incoming helicopter.

PRC-25 – Army radio carried on the back of an individual soldier or installed in a vehicle.

Push – Slang for *radio frequency.* The radio microphone is activated by pushing a switch, ergo the slang word *push.*

Ranger – *See US Army Ranger.*

Red Leg – The universal nickname for artillerymen derived from the red stripe that once adorned the outside seam of
each leg of an artilleryman's dress uniform trousers.

Roger – This word is used by military personnel on the radio to acknowledge that a transmission has been received and that it will be acted upon. Soldiers might say *Roger, Roger* for emphasis.

R&R – A common abbreviation for *rest and relaxation.*

RTO – Radio operator, derived from the job title *radio-telephone operator.*

Runner – Someone assigned to carry messages or run errands.

S-3 – The Personnel Officer is referred to as the S-1; Intelligence Officer as S-2; Operations Officer as S-3; and Supply Officer as S-4. *See Operations Officer.*

Second Lieutenant – See *US Army Officer Ranks.*

SITREP – Slang for situation report.

Squad – *See Army Unit.*

Tactical Operations Center (TOC) – The battalion level command center; the nerve center or war room of the battalion commander and staff that coordinate tactical operations, update the map of the battle front, and maintain communications with frontline units and support elements.

Three Bags Full – Slang words reinforcing a positive response to a question—derived from the children's poem "Black sheep, black sheep, have you any wool? Yes, Sir, yes Sir, three bags full."

TOC – S*ee Tactical Operations Center.*

Troop(s) – One or more soldiers.

Triple canopy jungle – Treetop growth at three distinct intervals.

US Army Officer Ranks –

   General – Four-star general.

   Lieutenant General – Three star general.

   Major General – Two-star general.

   Brigadier General – One-star general.

Colonel – The insignia represented by an eagle with spread wings. The rank usually associated with the commander of a US Army brigade consisting of several battalions of soldiers.

Lieutenant Colonel – The insignia represented by a silver oak leaf—the rank usually associated with the commander of a US Army battalion consisting of several companies.

Major – The insignia represented by a gold oak leaf—the rank usually associated with the executive officer of a battalion and the battalion operations officer.

Captain – The insignia represented by two parallel silver bars—the rank usually associated with commanders of frontline companies.

First Lieutenant – The insignia represented by a single silver bar—the rank usually associated with company level executive officers, the second in command of the company.

Second Lieutenant – The insignia represented by a single gold bar—the rank usually associated with the leader of frontline platoons.

US Army Ranger – US Army Rangers are America's most highly skilled, rigorously trained, elite soldiers.

VC Sympathizer – One who collaborated with the Viet Cong or NVA

Viet Cong (Also VC or Vietcong) – The rebel forces whose aim was to *liberate* the South Vietnamese from their duly elected political leadership and return the area to the control of the communist government of North Vietnam.

Ville – Slang for *village.*

Wimp – Weak, incompetent, malingering person.

XO – Executive Officer. (second in command)

- About The Author -

Dale Collie's military service as a US Army Ranger included command assignments in Europe and Vietnam. Following a yearlong period of recovery from combat wounds, he spent another ten years on active duty as an amputee. Among his medals for distinguished service is the Purple Heart, awarded to those wounded during wartime.

Sales and distribution management experience gained in Fortune 500 chemical and textile companies subsequently enabled Dale to guide a bankrupt charity into a highly successful $37 million operation in just seven years—sheltering the homeless, feeding the hungry, and assisting people in the former Soviet Union by creating jobs, providing orphanage relief and adoption services, operating the first-ever privately owned Christian youth camp in Ukraine, and facilitating other church outreach programs.

For his entrepreneurial achievements with these charitable efforts, Dale was identified by *Fast Company* magazine as one of America's Fast 50 innovative business leaders.

Academic achievements include a Bachelor of Science degree in Chemistry from Murray State University and a Master of Arts degree in English from Michigan State University.

He has taught at the United States Military Academy at West Point, New York; University of Kentucky, Indiana Wesleyan University

Dale lives high on a remote mountain in the Blue Ridge Mountains of North Carolina.

-Dale Collie's Presentations-
www.CourageBuilders.com

Programs designed to build courage in leaders and businesses include the following:

Discover the connection between
    —Bottom line, heath care, absenteeism, personnel turnover
    —Stress
    —Leadership

Gain —A new leadership perspective
    —Ability to see possibilities, not problems
    —A vision for success

Learn how to embrace change and persevere in the face of great odds.

Uncover seven essential building blocks of effective leadership - as taught to US Army Rangers.

Understand how top-notch leaders
    —Gain the confidence of others
    —Get team input
    —Overcome great obstacles

Learn how one company went from 35-85% of market share using the US Army's Principles of War.

Dale Collie uses the leadership skills of US Army Rangers to help key people succeed in tough times.

-What Clients Have to Say-

"Thank you for the outstanding program ... You had the keen ability to gauge the experience level of our team and ... tailored your program to fit ... Your conversational style ... made everyone feel comfortable. Your excellent storytelling ... was truly motivating." — William Walsh, FedEx

"I was struck by the startling parallels to the challenges we face in an ever increasingly difficult market. (Your) low key style moved a number of 'tough cookies' to reconsider their actions. Feedback from the senior team was positive ... a call to action was heard." — Kerri Boarman, Relizon

"I had no idea the profound effect this talk would have. You showed my employees the meaning of the term 'courage under fire' ... being able to foresee ambushes and cultivating an environment for success. Your use of Vietnam War experiences was riveting ... perfect for today's business world." — John Walvoord, Stratmark Corporation

"...your words of encouragement and your personal experience in overcoming change and seemingly insurmountable obstacles clearly inspired all of us." Karl Jacobs, Transcom

---

Dale Collie's journey from war room to boardroom speaks of boundless personal and professional success. He now invests his time showing others how to lead with courage.

186

-Other Books by Dale Collie-

Frontline Leadership: From War Room to Boardroom—True North Publishing

Winning Under Fire: Turn Stress into Success the US Army Way—McGraw-Hill Publishing

Campfires & Gun Smoke: Vietnam Company Commander – True North Publishing

Last Nerve: What's Driving Your Office Crazy and What to do About It – Create Space, Inc.

Contact Dale about working with your organization as a professional speaker—motivational or high content presentations.

Collie@CourageBuilders.com
www.CourageBuilders.com

-Order Information-

As a professional speaker, coach, and consultant, Dale Collie works with organizations that want to build courageous leaders and businesses.

Visit www.couragebuilders.com for information on how to:

> ➤ Contact Dale Collie as a speaker

> ➤ Order additional copies of this book or other Courage Builders products

> ➤ Find instructions for quoting or reprinting the contents of this book

> ➤ Find instructions for submitting your own stories for use in future books